BOOTS 2 BENEFITS:

OPERATION FUBAR

A TACTICAL GUIDE
TO ORGANIZING
YOUR DOCUMENTATION
FOR VA DISABILITY
BENEFITS

BOOTS 2
1
BENEFITS

SARGE J. MUSTER BRYSON

Library of Congress Control Number: 2025918528

Paperback ISBN: 978-1-969063-05-3
Hardcover ISBN: 978-1-969063-06-0

1. Main category—Nonfiction › Law › Specialties › Military
2. Other category—Nonfiction › Politics & Social Sciences › Politics & Government › Public Affairs & Policy › Social Services & Welfare
3. Other category—Nonfiction › Law › Specialties › Disability

AR
PRESS

Published by American Real Publishing
americanrealpublishing.com

DEDICATED TO MY BATTLE BUDDY, MANDA PANDA

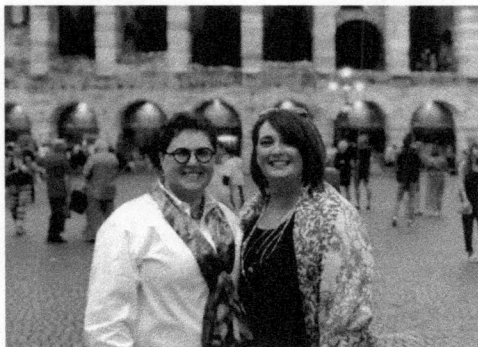

You've been my rock, my confidant, and my partner in crime through it all. From the trenches to the triumphs—from smelly feet in the pup tent to 18-mile ruck marches under the South Carolina sun—we've stood shoulder to shoulder, unwavering and true.

You're not just a friend—you're my ride or die, even if that means running out of gas on a motorcycle in the middle of Minnesota bear country (yeah, still not over that). The best adventures always come with a few unexpected detours, and let's be honest, we were never built for the straight road anyway. We will always be off-road or bust.

Your loyalty, your fire, and your unwavering support have made you more than a friend—you're my sister, plain and simple. Thank you for being my sounding board, my hype squad, my co-conspirator, and my forever firearms range buddy.

This book is dedicated to you for showing me what genuine friendship and family truly look like.

IGY6.2, whether you want it or not, always.

TABLE OF CONTENTS

Introduction vii

PART I: Troop Tasks 1

    Chapter 1: Check Your Gear 3

    Chapter 2: First Priorities 9

    Chapter 3: Who Will Submit My Claim? 20

    Chapter 4: You are your own warrior 25

PART II: Command Duties 31

    Chapter 5: Documentation & Medical Records 32

    Chapter 6: Take Charge AND Put the VA to work! 43

    Chapter 7: C&P Exams 48

PART III: Regulations & Tasks 57

    Chapter 8: Warrior's Guide 38 CFR 58

    Chapter 9: Nexus letters 62

    Chapter 10: Buddy Statements 68

PART IV: Operation Aftermath 73

    Chapter 11: Decision Letter 74

    Chapter 12: Appeal 76

PART V: TEAM IGY6.2 79

    Chapter 13: Military Sexual Trauma (MST) 81

    Chapter 14: Female Veterans 84

    Chapter 15: Catch All 88

Sample Templates 92

Nexus Letter Template 95

Vocabulary 98

Veterans helping Veterans 101

Feedback 104

Bonus Boots: Operation Extras 105

Epilogue 107

Acknowledgments 109

About the Author 111

INTRODUCTION

Welcome, Warrior!

Congratulations on taking your first step toward claiming the hard-earned benefits you rightfully deserve. Just opening this guide means you're already in the fight, and that's half the battle. What you're holding isn't just a book—it's years of blood, sweat, and VA-induced tears, written by someone who's been right there in the trenches.

I've always believed veterans are my family. We may have worn various patches, served on different soil, but we all signed the same dotted line—and that makes us brothers and sisters for life. That's why I created this guide, to help you make sense of the chaos and finally get what you deserve. If something's missing from this first book, or you've got a question I didn't answer, call, text, or email me—my contact info's on the last page. You won't find some call center—you'll find me, good ole' Sarge.

This isn't just about your individual claim—it's about the IGY6.2 Movement. 'I've Got Your 6' means we watch each other's backs, and that doesn't end when we hang up the uniform. Every veteran who successfully navigates this system becomes a battle buddy for the next one. When you get your back pay, when you finally get rated fairly, remember the veteran behind you who's just starting this fight. That's the IGY6.2 way—we lift each other up, we share our victories, and no veteran gets left behind.

I humbly offer this guide to you, the courageous souls who traded comfort for combat boots, who ran toward danger while others ran from it. You fought for America. And now? You're fighting a different kind of battle, one that requires forms, evidence, and a deep tolerance for red tape. But hear me when I say, you're battle-tested, and you absolutely can do this.

We've faced worse. We've made split-second decisions with lives on the line. Now we're being told to wait six to twelve months for a claim decision? Yeah, this fight's frustrating, but it's one we can win. And when some clueless civilian says, "Oh, you just want free money or health care," don't waste your breath. Smile, remind them that you fought for their right to run their mouth, and walk away with your head high. We already know what time it is.

I'm here to help you find your voice, understand the VA's foreign language, and lay out the step-by-step plan to get your claim submitted properly. Why? Because I spent 23 years stuck in the same VA maze, with three service-connected conditions rated at 0%. Why? Because I used common sense, and in the VA world, that's a tactical error. Trust me, you're going to have to unlearn some logic and dig deep into those medical records, because what you think matters might not be what they look for.

This is your call to action. And you better believe you'll hear stories, from the battlefield to the broken copier at the VA clinic. But that's what we do—we share, adapt, and overcome. Because in the veteran world, we stand on equal ground. Doesn't matter what your rank was. We all served, and we all sacrificed. We speak a language most civilians can't understand, but we understand each other, and that's what matters.

In uniform, we followed orders without question. But in the civilian and VA world, you've got the right to speak up, ask questions, and push back when something doesn't feel right. Many VA employees have never worn the uniform. They won't understand why you didn't go to sick call. They won't get why you "sucked it up and drove on." So, educate them. That's your right—you fought for it.

If you get a VA decision that doesn't sit right, challenge it. Appeal it. Fight back. You've got the right, and you've got the power to advocate for yourself. No one's going to fight harder for you than you, but I'm right here with you, every step of the way.

So now, I'm going to ask you to do something that might feel unnatural: Surrender to the VA's mysterious language. Learn the regs. Know the process. Embrace the suck, and let's take on this mission together—Operation FUBAR.

Let's get to work.

PART I: TROOP TASKS

As a veteran or service member trying to navigate civilian life, the benefits and claims process can feel like a full-blown recon mission without a map. The internet's swamped with advice. Some of it's good, a lot of it's junk, and most of it just leaves you wondering where to start, what to trust, and how to make sense of it all.

That's where Part One comes in. This section is your initial mission brief, the essential steps that'll get you squared away before filing a claim. If you complete these tasks, you'll walk into the VA fight with your ammo loaded—the right documentation, a solid understanding of your conditions, and a battle plan that makes the whole process smoother and a hell of a lot more successful.

Now I'm going to ask you to do something tough—surrender your common sense. Yeah, I said it. Because the VA doesn't run on logic. It runs on regs, language, and bureaucracy. So we're going to do it their way—and win.

Let's take this hill together, step-by-step. Welcome to Operation FUBAR.

CHAPTER 1: CHECK YOUR GEAR

Anticipating whether you should file a VA claim can feel like deciding to either dive into a pool of sharks or stick your eyeball with needles. This is something very personal, and you must choose when the time is right for you. But don't worry, you are not alone! We will figure this out together!

Listen up, troop.

Renting a car comes with rules, right? Before they toss you the keys, you walk around that thing with a clipboard, checking every scratch, every ding, every tiny chip in the paint. Why? Because when you bring it back, if there's a new dent—even one the size of a dime— they're going to hold you responsible. It doesn't matter if it was a pothole or a runaway shopping cart. It broke on your watch, so you have to fix it. Or more accurately, you pay for it. Before you think Sarge has lost her mind, just keep reading.

Now let's talk about your time in uniform.

When you raised your right hand and signed that enlistment contract, you were the government's shiny rental. Clean slate. If you had bad knees, asthma, or a busted back before, guess what? They wouldn't have let you in. They check. You passed MEPS (Military Entrance Processing Station). You passed their standards. You were mission capable.

But somewhere between basic training, deployments, ruck marches, jumping out of planes, working sixteen-hour shifts on the flight line, or getting thrown around in a Humvee, your "vehicle" took some damage. Now you're out, and the government doesn't get to just toss you the keys back and say, "Good luck."

Just like the rental company expects the car returned in one piece, Uncle Sam owes you for the wear and tear that happened on their watch.

So if your knees are shot, your hearing's gone, your back's jacked, or you've got nightmares that won't quit, you file. Because your body and your mind were loaned out in service to this country. You didn't break it—it broke during your service, which was the government's watch. Now, it's the VA's turn to fix it, heal it, address it, or manage it.

And here's the thing, when you finally get what you've earned, you'll understand why the IGY6.2 Movement matters. Because there's another veteran out there right now, staring at this same decision, wondering if they deserve help. They do. And when your claim comes through, you'll have the power to help them get theirs. That's what 'I've Got Your 6' really means.

Plain and simple, Soldier, you didn't start broken. You served your country and are battle-tested and worn. You sure as hell deserve to be made whole.

Step 1: Decades Have Passed. Can I Still File? Yes!

It doesn't matter how long you've been out of the service. You can file for VA disability!

1. VA Support: Even if you have been going to the VA hospital or clinic for decades to support the care of a disability or injury, that is completely different from filing for VA disability. The VA can/should utilize those records to support your claim.

2. Non-VA Support: If you have seen civilian doctors, gone to civilian medical centers or hospitals to treat ailments, injuries, or disability stemming from your service, you can still file a VA disability claim.

Step 2: Assess Your Situation

First, take a good, hard look at yourself (preferably in a mirror while striking a heroic pose). Humble yourself, Warrior! Kick the tires, and look for dings and dents!

1. Physical Ailments: Do you have aches and pains that make you groan louder than your grandparents? If you have injuries or conditions from your time in service, that's a solid reason to file.

2. Mental Health: Are your stress levels through the roof, or do you feel like you're constantly walking on eggshells? Service-related mental health conditions like PTSD (post-traumatic stress disorder) are valid reasons to file, even if you never sought medical while on active duty! Do you feel like you are misunderstood? Do civilians talk about your abrasive tongue? Do you feel like civilians just don't understand? All of these are side effects of military service.

3. Service Connection: Do you believe these issues are directly related to your military service? Perhaps, you're dealing with a secondary condition to your PTSD, e.g., Sleep Apnea, Narcolepsy, etc. You're on the right track!

4. The practical thing to do is to file. It won't hurt anything!

Step 3: Gather Intel

1. Talk to fellow veterans: Choose carefully. Some of them have been through it and might have some golden nuggets of wisdom! You want to find that veteran who wants to share VA disability claim war stories.

2. Research: Head to the VA website, veterans' forums, and do an internet search! Information is not just power; in this instance, it can also lead to lifelong resources for you and your family.

Step 4: Weigh the Pros and Cons

Time to play a little game of "Pros and Cons."

1. Pros:
2. You will potentially receive compensation.

   a. Access to VA health care and other benefits.
   b. Peace of mind knowing you're getting support for your service-related conditions.
   c. After a certain disability level (50%), your dependents start to get benefits, such as an ID card, and even at 100% P&T, they get health care!
   d. If you do attain 100% P&T, there are property tax exemptions, vehicle license savings, and other benefits, depending on the state in which you reside.
   e. At 100% P&T, your children will get college benefits (in addition to the GI Bill), and you can get your own student loans forgiven!
   f. Cons:
   g. The process can be slow.
   h. There's paperwork, lots of it.
   i. There is bureaucracy that will drive you up a wall!

j.   The mental exhaustion of having to re-live stressful experiences is a serious consideration. Make sure you have a support system, even if it is at the local American Legion, an online veteran forum, or even your dog, ferret, turtle, or cat!

Step 5: Make the Decision

Do what you usually do to make an important decision—even if it is just flipping a coin! More realistically, though:

1.   Think Long-Term: Consider how not filing could affect your health, mental well-being, and finances down the line.

2.   Seriously consider the impact on your mental well-being. As you navigate through this process, particularly if you must confront trauma, you will need to fortify your inner resolve to persevere and meet challenges head-on. *(I have suggestions on how it may be easier in Chapter 4.)*

3.   Get Support: Talk it over with family, friends, and other veterans you trust. Sometimes they see things more clearly than you do.

If you decide to file, remember you're not alone. Many of your fellow veteran brothers and sisters have navigated these waters before you and came out the other side. After the headaches and heartaches have passed, you may end up with hilarious stories of your bureaucratic battles. So, muster up that military grit and decide for you! And if you choose not to file, that's okay too. It's your decision, and you've earned the right to choose!

Remember, though, filing your claim isn't just about you. It's about proving the system works for all of us. Every successful claim makes it easier for the next veteran. Every time we stand up and say, "I served, I sacrificed, and I earned this," we're fighting for our entire military family.

If you're the kind of veteran who says, *"I'm fine, it's no big deal,"* or *"Other folks had it worse,"* stop right there. That humble, harmless attitude might serve you well in life, but it'll wreck your disability claim. The VA doesn't rate based on how tough you are. They rate based on how your conditions affect your daily life. If you downplay it, they'll underrate it—or worse, deny it. This is not the time to be quiet, modest, or "harmless." Be honest, humble yourself, and stop making excuses. Be detailed. Tell the truth, even when it's ugly. Because if you don't speak up for yourself, the system sure won't.

CHAPTER 2: FIRST PRIORITIES

It's time to roll up those sleeves and dive into the wonderful and dreadful world of your medical records. Yes, it might feel like deciphering ancient hieroglyphics, but trust me, it's worth it.

And remember, every veteran who masters this process becomes a battle buddy for the next one. That's the IGY6.2 way. When you finally get your rating and that back pay hits your account, you'll understand why helping other veterans navigate this maze matters so much. We're not just fighting for ourselves—we're paving the road for every veteran behind us.

Step 1: Set Up Your VA.gov Account

STOP WHAT YOU ARE DOING! Go to VA.gov and get your account created. **NOW!**

    a.   If you don't already have one, sign up and create your login.

    b.   If you have one, make sure it is working, *and* you can gain access to it! That means ensure you have your login and know your password. (It's against all things OPSEC [Operational Security], but write it down if you have to.) This website is your lifeline.

Step 2: Do You Have Your DD-214?

Confirm you have your DD-214 (Discharge from Active Duty) and that it is accurate.

    a.   If you do not have it, you will need to request a copy ASAP. You can do this from the va.gov website. *Helpful hint: keep records (email, confirmation, notes) of date, time, email, address, or telephone number that you contacted to request your records. You never know when you'll need it!

    b.   If you need to correct your DD-214, submit a Form DD-149 or DD Form 293 along with your current DD-214. All forms can be found at va.gov and the https://boots2benefits.com/resources website.

        Once it is corrected, you'll get a DD-215.

    c.   A veteran can file his/her DD-214 at the local court-house, but please realize that it then becomes a public document.

Step 3: Submit an Intent to File.

    a.   You have one (1) year from your submission of an Intent to File to provide all the documentation for your claim(s). *If you do not know the exact name of the ailment(s) yet, do not list it.* (By exact name, I mean what it is called in your service medical record.) Typically, your back pay date for said ailment(s) is the date you submitted your intent to file. It is in your best interest to submit it as soon as possible.

    b.   Heads up, back pay isn't just a financial transaction – although receiving it is often a very nice surprise! It is your power to help other veterans. Through the IGY6.2 Fund, which provides financial assistance to veterans who can't afford VA claim guidance but desperately need it. Every dollar you contribute helps a veteran receive that professional guidance. That's how we take care of our own.

Step 4: Gather Your Medical Records.

This is a lot of red tape, but it is necessary (mandatory, nonnegotiable) and worth it!

Think of this as assembling your own personal library of "What FUBAR action caused me to get this way" documentation. You'll need:

1. Service Treatment Records: These are the chronicles of every time you visited the medic or doctor while in service.

    a. If you were 'in the heat of battle' and a medic took care of it but didn't have the ability to memorialize it in writing, it is okay. This is where buddy statements or campaign documentation come into your corner to support your claim.

    b. If you were stationed somewhere and had to go to a civilian doctor or hospital (example: to have a baby, surgery), ensure you get those medical records, lab slips, and documents too.

2. VA Medical Records: If you've been treated at a VA facility, grab these from that records department.

3. Private Medical Records: Don't forget any treatments you received outside the VA system. This includes any emergency room or urgent care visits!

4. Gather it all: You'll be surprised at things a doctor wrote down but did not tell you!

Step 5: Review All Records/Documents with a Fine-Tooth Comb!

Channel your inner reconnaissance fighter. This is for your benefit—it's okay to put yourself first!

1. Read everything: Don't skip anything, even if it looks boring. That scribbled note might be the key to your claim!

    I found a priceless written item on my DD 4/1 initial recruitment document from the MEPS (Military Entrance Processing Station). Someone wrote that I was mentally cleared to serve. (I share this from experience. I had a traumatic childhood, but it clearly stated on my initial contract that I was cleared to serve.)

    a. Since I hadn't reported my PTSD during my active-duty tenure, this was a crucial piece of evidence.
    b. Trust me, look over everything! Or have a trusted person help you look at all of it!

2. Coordinate the details: Look for mentions of your conditions, treatments, and any statements linking your ailments to your service. This is going to be work, but create a written list or a typed spreadsheet of your ailments!

Step 6: Create a Spreadsheet of Your Ailments.

It's time to get organized. Open up Excel, Google Sheets, or grab a good old-fashioned notebook. Create a spreadsheet so you can sort it by ailment, duty location, or dates!

1. List each ailment *exactly* as the doctor wrote it. No creative interpretations. If it says,

"patellofemoral pain syndrome," write that, not "swollen knee."

    a.   But add a column for "Details" and put your "swollen knee during rescue swimmer training" note or incident information there.

    b.   Also, even if the doctor called it arthritis when you were speaking to them, if that isn't what is written in your file, list it as it is written! (Take it from me!)

2.   Include dates: What date were you seen by the military clinic professional for this ailment? If you have the information, what date did it start? (Estimate, even if it is just one week, e.g., prior in the field, I tripped over a log…) When was it diagnosed? Every date is important.

3.   Duty location: Where were you stationed or deployed when this happened? Context matters—if you were at sea and you don't remember what waters you were in, write down the name of the submarine, etc.!

Pro tip: Once you've mastered this spreadsheet system, pass it on—become invaluable to other veterans. Share your knowledge. Help a battle buddy organize their records. That's IGY6.2 in action—using your hard-won expertise to lift up another veteran. We're stronger when we fight together.

Step 7: Cross-Reference with Your Service Records.

Connect the dots between your ailments and your service.

1. Service connection: Try to link each ailment to a specific event or duty period. This is crucial for your claim.

2. If you have ailments that have worsened, especially those that can be linked to environmental issues—the water, ordnance, chemicals, etc.—research your duty locations and the local environment testing results! Endocrinological disorders can be brought on by environmental issues.

3. You need to take a deep dive and read about TERA (Toxic Exposure Risk Assessment) and the PACT (Promise to Address Comprehensive Toxics) Act for Veterans. Check out the example of an environmental impact letter in Chapter 15.

Bottom line, if you served and smelled the burn pit smoke, breathed in jet fuel fumes, or stood post next to God-knows-what toxic mess, the TERA and PACT Act are your battle plan. TERA is the VA's way of finally asking the right question: *"Were you exposed?"* Here's your chance to document every nasty thing you were exposed to during service, whether you realized it was hazardous at the time or

not. Then there's the PACT Act, which kicks the doors wide open. It gives you the upper hand by recognizing presumptive conditions, meaning you don't have to prove the VA's usual ridiculous burden of evidence. These laws are the ammo you need to fight back for the benefits and health care you *earned*.

And remember, these are all different pots of money.

1. The Burn Pit Registry is different than the VA Disability claim.

2. The PACT Act registry is different than a VA Disability.

3. With your spreadsheet, your ailments/conditions/sicknesses will become apparent, and you file for those—all of them! Even if you think it's trivial, ailments tend to worsen with age. You don't want to deal with a health crisis *and* contend with a claim regarding this VA disability at the same time.

All right, listen up, Soldier, it's time to drag out that *ugly black military binder*—yeah, the one with the busted rings and plastic sheet protectors that smell like chow hall mystery meat, you know the one. Inside that binder is your ammo: orders, evals, award memos, deployment rosters, medical records—you name it. Don't just flip through it like you're reminiscing about old war stories. Comb through every page like you're clearing a room for the safety of your squad. You're looking for proof—dates, units, locations, anything that backs up where you were and what you did. If you see a TDY (temporary duty) order to a toxic hotspot, a deployment award, or sick call slips from the middle of a sandstorm, you hold onto that like it's classified intel. That binder might be a mess, but buried in there is gold—the evidence that could win your claim. So dig in, Soldier. Victory's in the details.

1. I realize that this type of detailed task isn't everyone's cup of tea. So, if it's not in your wheelhouse, hire someone to do it for you. It's just cut and paste from one document to

a spreadsheet. Then *you* can fill in the details after it's complete! (Boots 2 Benefits has a list of people to assist you!)

Step 8: Double-Check for Consistency.

Ensure that what's in your medical records matches up with your spreadsheet. *Any* discrepancies can (and will) slow down your claim process. Make your own notes, even if it is just a definition of what the doctor wrote—anything for it to jog your memory when questioned about it during an exam.

1. This is where your war stories become evidence, not just barstool legends. You start with: "We were in that rice paddy in the Mekong Delta with Sergeant Buckteeth, and he forced us to stay in that slimy, smelly creek with the human waste for three hours as punishment for not changing out our wool socks."

2. That isn't just a memory—that's context. It was hot, so it had to be June or July. You remember because you were sweating through your BDUs and your boots felt like microwaves. "I was with Corporal Munson and both of us started throwing up." *Boom*—that's a service-connected event tied to a place, a time, symptoms, and witnesses.

3. The VA wants timelines, locations, and symptoms. We know, so you better grab those stories, dust 'em off, and turn 'em into claims gold. This is how you prove it happened. This is how you win.

Step 9: Prepare Your Evidence.

When you file your claim, evidence will have to be provided. Being organized now will save you a ton of headaches later.

1. If you choose to get your own medical records, submit copies. *Never send original documents.* Always submit copies and keep the originals safe.

2. Clear Explanations—think of KISS (Keep It Simple Stupid; no offense)!

   a. When you submit your claim, I recommend including a cover letter (example in Chapter 15) outlining the information from your spreadsheet so the VA can clearly see how your medical (or personnel) records support your claim for service connection.

   b. Remember how you felt when you looked at all those documents and thought, *Holy crap, that's a lot!* The VA contractors and workers are thinking the same thing. So, make it dummy-proof for their sake! You have done the work, and this is for your benefit. Just tell them where it is in your medical or personnel record(s)! And once again, when you finally win your claim using these tactics, don't keep the victory to yourself. Share your success story. Help another veteran understand the process. That's what the IGY6.2 Movement is all about—veterans helping veterans, one claim at a time. Because when one of us wins, we all win.

3. Although I eventually received my military medical records, I had to request them multiple times. When I contacted my veteran-friendly senator and gave his staff a signed release (and my two other documents when I asked for my records in the official way). I had them within ten days! We all know

this isn't right. If you don't receive them in a timely manner, try this tactic!

4. Missing records are not your fault!

    a. On July 12, 1973, a fire broke out in the National Personnel Records Center in St. Louis, Missouri. This fire destroyed approximately 16-18 million Official Military Personnel Files (OMPFs).

    b. If the response is that they cannot find your records, see the detailed steps on page 24 for how to "recreate them."

5. Note: Since you will be going off your memory, this may need to be done and revisited later. You may recall other details out of nowhere. Or your spouse, mom, or battle buddy may recall the story and have details you'd forgotten.

    Take notes for everything, "I was with Bob in the tank attack at Arras in May 1940, tagging along with the Brits. That one toothless guy (with the funny name from Iowa) was nearby. That's when we got that downpour of rain, and I got pneumonia."

6. To get my civilian medical records, I gave all my civilian physician details to the VA, so the VA requested my civilian medical records.

    a. For me, this was the best course of action because the VA got a quicker response because they gave a deadline.

    b. The VA also pays the fees to get copies of the records.

    c. Plus, the VA is very communicative with you (every two weeks or so) as to which doctors' offices are not complying with the request so that you can step in!

    d. This is especially important if you are female and you had a different last name during your service.

Take this time to care for yourself. Remember that getting your documentation together for your VA disability claim is like basic training. If you don't get it together now, you'll be doing extra ~~firewatch~~ paperwork for the rest of your life! Let's turn that chaos into a solid battle plan.

CHAPTER 3: WHO WILL SUBMIT MY CLAIM?

Every veteran has several options of who can help submit his/her disability claim. I did it myself with the help of a DAV (Disabled American Veterans) representative to decipher the convoluted VA language. I sought out fellow veterans who had already been through the process, and I took a 30-minute seminar by a highly acclaimed VSO (Veterans Service Officer) who runs a private Veteran Facebook page. With all of this support, I still did plenty of internet searches on all the different ailments, forms, and documentation! Hence, I'm here to share this experience with you so you can make the best choice for you.

The most common choices to submit your claim are as follows:

1. Submit it yourself through www.va.gov.

2. Find a Veteran Services Officer to do it on your behalf. By law, VSOs and VSO representatives cannot charge a fee to put in a claim on your behalf.

    a. VSOs operate at a national, regional, state, and local level.

        I. Local VSOs can be found at your county government or veteran organizations

        II. State government

        III. Federal government (such as at the VA)

        IV. Veteran Organizations: DAV, American Legion, etc. These are volunteers.

V.   As with any profession, there are good and bad VSOs. Ask fellow veterans who they would recommend. Interview them or ask questions. The person you pick will speak on your behalf.

When you're picking a VSO, don't just settle for the first name in the phone book or the guy handing out brochures at the VFW (Veterans of Foreign Wars). You want someone who acts like they're still on a mission—timely, squared away, and knows the terrain. If they take two weeks to answer a simple question or can't explain what a Nexus letter is, walk away. You need someone who picks up the phone, calls you back, and makes you feel like your claim matters to them. They should know VA regs, deadlines, and what to do when your claim goes sideways. A good VSO doesn't talk down to you or shrug their shoulders—they break it down, guide you through, and have your back every step of the way. You fought too hard to get here. Make daggone sure they fight just as hard for you.

b.   You can call 888-777-4443 to ask where to find a VSO in your local area. Also, va.gov has a list of approved organizations with VSOs.

1.   Hire a private attorney.

a.   Please allow me to give you a little advice. Attorneys will typically take part of your VA back pay— 20-33%! However, no attorney can charge you more than 33.33% of your retroactive benefits for their services.

b.   When you're deep in appeal territory, an attorney may be necessary. But let's be real—they take up to 33.33% of your back pay. That's a big chunk of money you bled for.

c.   Ask yourself: Is your timeline their priority? The longer they take, the more back pay you get, and that means a bigger paycheck for them! You may be one of a hundred files on their desk. Before handing over that kind of cut, try a trusted VSO or accredited advocate who won't charge you a dime. Save the big guns for when/if you need 'em, so you can keep more of what you earned.

d. Here's Sarge's advice: Exhaust every free resource first. Use VSOs, DAV, AMVETS, your battle buddies, or heck, call *me*. Keep that money where it belongs—in your pocket, not their vacation fund. You already paid in blood, sweat, and broken knees. Don't pay again by handing over 1/3 of your back pay.

Conduct your reconnaissance! If you choose to select option two or three above, this person will speak for you. Their words will carry weight with the VA, just as if you are talking!

Circumstances: The veteran may have unique circumstances, depending on his/her health status, financial situation, and support network, that give him/her priority and expedited processing of a disability claim.

1. Financial: The VA will look for foreclosure notices, past-due utility bills, and collection attempts.

2. Health:

    a. If the veteran is terminally ill, it will require the submission of medical documentation.

    b. Serious injury will also require the submission of medical documentation.

3. Homelessness: This is not the time to "suck it up and drive on." If you're homeless or at risk of becoming homeless, the VA has a process to get your disability claim moved to the front of the line. It's called priority or expedited processing, and it's there for a reason. No veteran should be sleeping in a car, living in a hotel, or on the street while waiting months

for a decision. You or your advocate just need to submit a statement saying you're homeless or provide documentation like a shelter intake letter. The VA will flag your file and push it through faster. So don't wait. Raise your hand, speak up, and demand the support you've earned. Hard times don't mean you're alone or that you have failed somehow. Let's get you and yours housed and healed.

Obstacles: If you're filing for trauma-related claims (PTSD [post-traumatic stress disorder], MST[military sexual trauma], or any service-connected mental health condition), you need to know this path may come with some extra weight. For my MST survivors, I see you. I hear you. If you didn't report it at the time, that does not mean it didn't happen. Before you ask, yes, I have helped a male veteran submit (and win) his MST claim. The same goes for PTSD. Regardless of whether it came from combat, loss, an accident, or something that still wakes you up at night, your experience is real, and it deserves to be heard and respected.

This is where your buddy statements, Nexus letters, and other supporting evidence become your weapon loadout. You're building a case that tells the truth of your story in a way the VA can understand—and that means documentation matters, even when the pain goes far deeper than paper can show.

You are a warrior. If this was easy, everyone would do it. But you? You signed that dotted line. You served. You endured. You've already proven you've got what it takes. And yeah, this claim might mean a few more battles before victory. But I believe in you. I know what you're made of.

So stand firm. Stick to your battle plan. And never forget, you're not alone in this fight. Stay the course. Remember, this isn't just about your individual fight. Every veteran who successfully navigates this system using these strategies proves it can be done. You're not just claiming your benefits, you're lighting the way for every veteran who comes after you. That's your mission now: get what you've earned, then help others do the same. IGY6.2, always.

CHAPTER 4: YOU ARE YOUR OWN WARRIOR

No One takes care of you like *you* do!

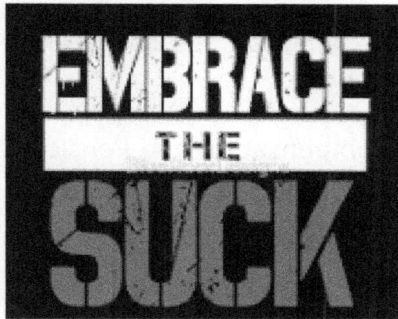

Do yourself a favor: complete the foundation work regardless of whom you select to file your disability claim. Once you master this process, you become part of something bigger. The IGY6.2 Movement isn't just about getting your own benefits. It's about every veteran who comes after you. When you figure out how to navigate this VA system of bureaucracy, you become a battle buddy for the next veteran who's staring at these same forms, feeling overwhelmed. That's what 'I've Got Your 6' really means.

Here's the deal: if you've served, you deserve to get the benefits you're entitled to because you *earned* them.

Here's a quick guide to get you started:

Step 1: Embrace the Adventure

Think of filing a VA claim as a mission. Your mission is to secure the benefits you've *earned*. Arm yourself with the proper weapons: patience, persistence, information, and a high-speed internet connection.

Never forget, every successful claim you file proves the system works. You're not only fighting for yourself, you're proving it can be done for every veteran watching from the sidelines, wondering if they should file too.

Step 2: Learn to Speak VA

Yes, the VA has its own language. It's kind of like learning Klingon but potentially more useful.

1. C&P Exam: Compensation and Pension Exam. Think of it as your chance to show off your battle scars (literal or meta-phorical), so always be prepared for a physical exam.

2. NOD: Notice of Disagreement. It's what you file if the VA's decision wasn't fair or appropriate.

3. Service-Connected: This means your condition is directly related to your military service. The VA loves this term, so get comfy with it and remember you "want" the service-connected designation.

4. Secondary Service-Connected Disability: This is something you developed that was caused by a service-connected dis-ability. For example, you already have service-connected PTSD, and now you've developed sleep apnea, though you didn't report it when you were on active duty.

   a. You're snoring like a chainsaw, waking up gasping, or using a CPAP just to survive the night. That isn't just getting older—it could be directly tied to your PTSD. It doesn't matter that you did not go to sick call about it while on active duty; if you don't claim it, you're leaving benefits on the battlefield. Trust me, your tent buddy remembers your insane snoring! Get that buddy statement.

Step 3: Get Your Ducks in a Row

It's time to gather intel (information) for your battle plan. Only, this battle is about how you hurt your back jumping out of airplanes, or got shin splints running in your new boots, or how the chemicals in the water at Camp Lejeune messed up your endocrine system.

1. Service Records: They proved you were there, did that, and got the T-shirt.

2. Medical Records: Every doctor's visit, every prescription, every little "ouch" and "ugh" that was documented. The VA loves details. (And it is up to you to tell the VA where to find the details, aka, evidence!)

Step 4: File That Claim

It's time to take the hill! Head to the VA's website and start your claim. Yes, it's a bit like navigating an online maze, but it is all there!

1. VA Form 21-526EZ: This is your main form. Please fill it out as completely as possible. Use the *exact word* that is written in your medical records, even if your civilian doctors have narrowed an ailment more specifically.

    a. For instance, if the military doctor stated you had a thyroid condition, but your civilian doctor says you have a hypothyroid condition. File for the *military* doctor's term for thyroid condition!

2. Buddy Statements: If you've got battle buddies, colleagues, family, or friends who were there with you, saw the injury, heard about the harassment, or witnessed the psychological harm since 'something' happened, ask them to write a statement. They can fill out the VA Form 21-4138. However,

the buddy can just type it/write it out on paper and just have their signature notarized. This is especially helpful for those times when you got hurt or ill and you didn't have time to seek medical care during battle, so it hit you later on.

a. Never forget you're part of something powerful. When you get those buddy statements, you're already living the IGY6.2 philosophy. Your battle buddy is literally 'having your six' by documenting your service experiences and supporting your claim.

b. When you successfully use those statements to win your benefits, you become the veteran who can write powerful buddy statements for others.

That's how the IGY6.2 Movement grows—one statement at a time, one veteran supporting another, continuing the brotherhood and sisterhood that started in uniform. Your success with buddy statements becomes someone else's roadmap to victory.

3. Bottom line, we were all in the military, and we know that you heard "Suck it up and drive on!" a million times! You file what you feel is your injury or ailment. It will just have to be supported in other ways, e.g., buddy statements, an MRI showing an old partially torn Achilles tendon, etc.

Step 5: The Wait!

Now comes the hardest part: Waiting. It's easier to write that word than to do it! You can drive yourself nuts if you check the va.gov website every day! The VA will get back to you... eventually, do yourself a favor and be on a check-in schedule, such as every other Friday. The VA has up to a year to reply from the submission claim date.

Step 6: Thoroughly Review Your Decision Letter!

When the VA finally responds, read their decision letter carefully. If you're happy, congrats! If not, remember the NOD (Notice of Disagreement) I mentioned? Time to get comfortable with telling the VA you disagree! They need to review the decision based on your collection of data. Now, get out that spreadsheet and identify all the times the military doctor saw you, tested you, or treated you for the ailment, then detail it all in your appeal!

Step 7: Excessive Waiting

If your wait has become excessive, there are ways you can check up on your claim other than just checking the website. For example, if you had a C&P exam five months ago and they haven't made a decision, you can make some calls or send emails!

1. Call your Local Veterans Administration.

2. Call 'the' federal Veterans Administration at 800-827-1000,

    a. Keep detailed notes of when you called (date and time), whom you spoke with, and what they said.

    b. Add a tab to your spreadsheet just for "Communication with the VA" audit trail!

If that doesn't work, take it a step further!

1. Call the White House Veterans Administration at 855-948-2311.

2. Email or call your local veteran-friendly senators and/or congressman! They probably have staff specifically to assist veterans!

Final Pep Talk:

You've navigated tougher terrain than this. Remember those long rucksack marches? Filing a VA claim is just another mission, and you are tough enough to meet this head-on. So, let's learn the process, speak the VA language, and just get 'er done!

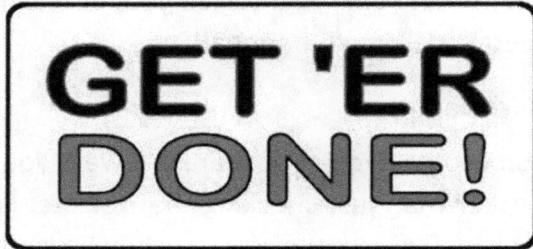

GET 'ER DONE!

PART II: COMMAND DUTIES

We know this, I know! There's always a Chain of Command, and in this context, your primary authority is the VA. Numerous individuals will be involved in processing your claim and supporting it. Let's break down whom you need to rely on for support, how to communicate effectively with them to receive exactly what you need, plus other items you should gather to ensure your claim is successfully processed.

Don't forget, every piece of documentation you gather, every record you organize, every Nexus letter you perfect isn't just building your personal case. You're creating a blueprint for the next veteran who walks this path. In the true IGY6.2 philosophy, you become the battle buddy who can guide others through the same fight.

CHAPTER 5: DOCUMENTATION & MEDICAL RECORDS

Follow-up is crucial for strengthening your VA disability claim. Civilian medical records can provide additional documentation and evidence to support your disability claim.

Step 1: Schedule Appointments with Civilian Doctors

If you haven't already, make appointments with civilian health care providers to treat your service-related conditions.

1. Civilian medical opinions can provide a crucial third-party perspective on your ailments.

2. Submitting another (or several) doctors who have treated your ailment is even more proof that the ailment has existed since you've exited the service. You've spent your valuable time and money trying to address it.

A really positive thing to focus on is that when you finally get your rating and that back pay comes through, you can help other veterans access this same level of care. The IGY6.2 Fund exists because not every veteran can afford multiple civilian doctors' visits. Your success today could fund another veteran's medical documentation tomorrow.

Step 2: Communicate Clearly with Your Doctor

When you visit your civilian doctor, if you haven't discussed it, explain your military service and clearly inform them that your ailments are related to your service.

1. Describe symptoms and history: Provide a detailed history of your symptoms, treatments received during service, after-service civilian care, and any previous diagnoses.

2. Explain that the VA will use their medical records to support your continued treatment for the service-connected ailment.

Step 3: Get Comprehensive Medical Documentation (or have the VA request it)

Ask your civilian doctor to provide detailed documentation of your conditions. Make sure the records include:

1. Diagnosis: Clear identification of each ailment.

2. Medical History: A thorough history of your condition(s), including when they began and how it has progressed.

3. Treatment Records: Details of any treatments or therapies you've received.

4. Nexus Letter: This letter is the medical evidence your doctor prepares for you that explains how and why the veteran's current medical condition is related to his/her military service or secondary to an established service-connected disability. It is a critical component of your claim.

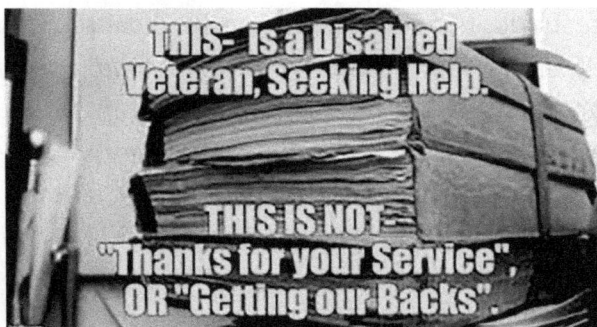

THIS- is a Disabled Veteran, Seeking Help.

THIS IS NOT "Thanks for your Service", OR "Getting our Backs".

5.   Be considerate of your physician's schedule by drafting the Nexus letter for his/her review. It is to your benefit, trust me; read below.

   a.   Start by doing your research in 38 CFR (Code of Federal Regulations). Get the symptoms directly from this regulation to support the civilian doctor's diagnosis. Rarely will the civilian doctor know what phrases and/or symptoms need to be included in the Nexus letter.

   b.   Double-check your Nexus letter for mistakes or ambiguous language. The doctor doesn't have to be 100% certain that it is service-connected. The Nexus letter physician's statement is "it is at least as likely as not that the veteran's [condition] is related to their military service." (This is another reason to draft your own Nexus letter for the physician only to have to edit.)

   c.   If it can be avoided, do not use a physician's assistant.

   d.   If there is a conflict in verbiage, the VA will use the downgraded choice.

Let me give you a real-world example of how one tiny mistake can cost you big! I assisted a veteran who served as a rescue swimmer—yeah, one of those warriors diving into chaos to save lives. He had a solid service-connected PTSD rating, and like many, developed sleep apnea as a secondary condition. He had medical records, the CPAP, and the sleep study that all clearly showed *mildly severe* obstructive sleep apnea. But when the physician assistant wrote the Nexus letter, she accidentally called it "mild." That one word—just one—was all the VA needed to deny the claim. They ignored the actual sleep study results and latched onto that word like a pit bull on a pork chop.

Here's the kicker, "midly severe" is still severe, which is a whole category above "mild." It isn't even close. But the VA doesn't fill in gaps or ask for clarification. If the paperwork is wrong, you lose. That's why every form, every diagnosis, and every Nexus letter has to be locked tight. No guesswork. No vague language. No typos. Because one slip of the pen can mean months—or years—of denied benefits, double-check everything like your life depends on it.

Step 4: Medical Records

You (or the VA) have requested copies of your medical records. You *need* copies of these records, too. Having these records on hand is crucial for your VA claim preparation. If you choose to do it yourself, here's what you need to do:

1. Request Full Records (C-File): Ensure you get complete records, including all notes, test results, and imaging studies.

2. Check for Accuracy: Review the records to ensure they accurately reflect your conditions and the discussions you had with your doctors.

3. Don't allow the VA to tell you that they have your military medical records, so you do not need a copy of them. *You have a right to have a copy.* They do not have the right to deny your request. You need to know precisely what the military physician or professionals said, the official diagnosis, test results, and so forth.

Step 5: Authorize the VA to Obtain Additional Records

If you prefer, you can authorize the VA to obtain your civilian medical records directly from your civilian doctors. To do this:

1. Fill out VA Form 21-4142: This form authorizes the release of your medical information to the VA.

2. Fill out VA Form 21-4142a: This form provides additional information about your health care providers.

Submit these forms with your claim so the VA can request the records on your behalf.

Seeing a civilian doctor for your military ailments is a smart move that can significantly strengthen your VA disability claim. Their records provide independent verification of your conditions and can help establish the necessary connection to your service. So, make those appointments, see the doctor, get detailed documentation, and make sure your civilian medical records are part of your claim. This will provide you with the strongest possible case for receiving the benefits you deserve.

Again, let the VA do some of the heavy lifting! Here's how you can make sure they handle the grunt work while you focus on getting your claim together. This approach can save you time and money, as the VA will take care of obtaining your civilian medical records and paying any associated fees with copying or transmitting the records to the VA.

Here's how:

1.   Fill out the authorization form, VA Form 21-4142:

     a.   Download and complete this form, "Authorization to Disclose Information to the Department of Veterans Affairs (VA)."

     b.   You'll need to list each health care provider who has treated you during and since the end of your service. Be thorough!

1.   Fill out the companion form, VA Form 21-4142a:

     a.   Also, complete this form, "General Release for Medical Provider Information to the Department of Veterans Affairs (VA)." It is used to list additional providers if you run out of space on the first form.

Work smart, not hard. By authorizing the VA to obtain your civilian medical records, you're making the process smoother for yourself and ensuring that the VA covers any associated costs. This strategy leverages the VA's resources and helps streamline your claim. So, take a deep breath, sign the release, and let the VA do some of the work. You've got this!

Step 6: Submit a *copy* of the records to the VA (only if you took the steps to get copies personally and not through the VA)

When you're ready to file your claim, include these civilian medical records as part of your evidence. This will help substantiate your claims and provide a comprehensive picture of your health. *If you have the VA request your records, you will not need to take this step.*

Step 7: How do you reconstruct your military records if your records were destroyed in the National Personnel Records Center (NPRC) in St. Louis?

The 1973 fire that destroyed records held for veterans who were discharged from the Army and Air Force during specific periods of time can complicate things. If your records were destroyed in this fire (or just plain lost), you are not without hope. Below are guidelines on how to reconstruct your records to support a VA claim.

Exactly what records were destroyed in the fire?

1. If you were in the Army between November 1, 1912, and January 1, 1960, the fire destroyed 80% of those records for veterans discharged from the Army during that period. The fire did <u>not</u> destroy records for retirees and reservists who were alive on July 12, 1973.

2. If you were in the Air Force between September 25, 1947, and January 1, 1964, the fire destroyed 75% of the records for veterans discharged from the Air Force during this period

of time with the surnames beginning with 'Hubbard' and running through the end of the alphabet.

Step 8: How does a veteran get the VA to reconstruct their records?

1. The VA submits a request to the NPRC for any additional service records that they may have or can find for you.

2. With the information you provide, the NPRC searches for documents that may help to reconstruct your records. They will also reach out to other government agencies. For example, they may try to reconstruct portions of your service treatment records by reviewing unit records, morning reports, and hospital admissions records from the Surgeon General's office.

Step 9: Submit a form to the National Archives.

You need to fill out a request for information needed to reconstruct medical data (NA Form 13055). Get the form from the VA website or the www.boots2benefits.com/tactical-tools website. They will use this form to request the NPRC to reconstruct your records as well.

1. The information that a veteran needs to supply is:
   a. Unit
   b. Company
   c. Battalion
   d. Regiment
   e. Squadron
   f. Group
   g. Wing

This is when you start making a list of the guys you served with—even if you only remember the short, blond guy from Idaho. It only takes one other person to ask, and he'll remember it was Wade "Bull's-eye" Tucker who fixed everything with duct tape.

I know you might not remember every detail, and shoot, I sure don't either. But here's what you can do: Go grab that big, ugly, black career binder—you know the one you've been dragging around since basic, with papers shoved in every direction like a tornado hit a personnel office. Start digging. Go through those orders, evals, medical sheets, and leave forms. Somewhere in that mess are the answers to the questions the VA's going to ask. It might take a little time, but remember, this benefits *you*. And if it feels overwhelming, ask for help. There are folks (like me) who can help you sort that chaos into mission-ready categories, so when it's time to file, you're locked, loaded, and ready to fire.

Andnever forget, once you've mastered the art of reconstructing records, you become invaluable to other veterans facing the same challenge. The IGY6.2 Movement is built on veterans helping veterans navigate these exact situations. Your hard-won expertise can become someone else's lifeline.

Check your personal files for documents that you may have that will be useful to help recreate your records.

1. Statements from service medical personnel.

2. Buddy statements are affidavits from fellow service members (or an acquaintance) who witnessed your injury, illness, or the side effects. The buddy's signature must be notarized. (Every bank has a notary!)

3. Military accidents and/or police records.

4. Examination reports related to employment or insurance.

5. Letters or photographs from your time in the service.

6. Prescription records.

7. Photocopies of any service treatment records or medical reports from a private hospital, clinic, or doctor who treated

you during service or shortly after your separation from service.

8. You can research records at the National Archives at: https://www.archives.gov/st-louis/other-records to attempt to find what you need.

9. Morning reports, unit, rosters, pay cards from WWI and WWII.

10. Remember that no one can take care of you like *you* can.

11. How do I submit my form and supporting documents?

   a. You can file your claim online at va.gov, by mail, in person, or with the help of a trained professional.

   b. Make sure that you include any supplemental records or other documents that you found (from the list above) with your NA Form 13055 submission.

   c. Mailing address: (Pay for the signed delivery receipt!)

   National Archives and Records Administration

   8601 Adelphi Road

   College Park, Maryland, 20740-6001

Let's break this beast down, Sarge-style! Your Official Military Personnel File is your military paper trail—your proof you served, what you did, where you went, and who you were when you wore the uniform. This file includes everything from your enlistment orders to your duty stations, awards, evals, training, and that golden ticket of proof: your DD-214. That document alone can open doors to VA benefits, health care, jobs, home loans, and veteran discounts at your favorite greasy spoon. So if you've been separated from service, your files are stored with the National Archives and Records Administration (NARA), not in some black hole.

Now, listen, don't sit around waiting for someone to read your mind. If you need your records, you've got options:

1. Use the eVetRecs system. It's online and the fastest.
2. Or print, sign, and mail or fax a Standard Form SF-180.

Just remember, if your DD-214 says "Honorable" and your records are squared away, you're already halfway through the gate. But if they're not? It's on you to dig it up. And if your binder looks like it exploded after a PCS (Permanent Change of Station)? Ask for help. A trusted advocate, VSO (Veterans Service Organization) representative, or Sarge can help you organize it into a mission-ready file. Bottom line: you earned that paperwork. Make sure it works *for* you, not against you.

And one more thing, don't expect your battle history or combat stories to be in those records. The VA doesn't include "that time we got lit up outside Baghdad" in your personnel file. So, you may need to back it up with buddy statements, awards citations, or deployment rosters.

Don't forget, every document you gather, every record you organize, every Nexus letter you perfect is ammunition not just for *your* fight, but for every veteran who comes after you. When you win your claim using these strategies, don't keep the victory to yourself. Share your knowledge. Help another veteran understand the process. That's the IGY6.2 way—we succeed together, and no veteran gets left behind.

Now go find that paper trail. It's the key to your benefits.

COMMUNICATE, COMMUNICATE, COMMUNICATE!

Let all of your civilian doctors know that a VA request for records is coming shortly.

If you are a female with a different last name than when you were serving, tell the doctor's office staff. (Several times and to various staff, if needed.)

The VA is very good at keeping you informed of which offices have or have not provided your records. Please keep checking in with the doctor's office staff until it is done. This is for *you*!

CHAPTER 6: TAKE CHARGE AND PUT THE VA TO WORK!

Submitting your intent to file a VA claim was a crucial step. Now, we will go into more detail about putting the VA to work for you! Here's the thing: when you finally master this documentation system and win your claim, you become the veteran who can teach others this critical skill. The IGY6.2 Movement thrives on veterans sharing these hard-won lessons. Your meticulous record-keeping today becomes someone else's roadmap tomorrow.

Bottom line up front: I've created a quick and fun guide on how to get moving in the right direction.

Step 1: Finish the Claim That You Already Started

Submitting your intent to file is like staking your claim in the VA's territory signaling, "Hey, I'm on it. Remember me!" This action secures your effective date, which is the date the VA will typically use to determine when your benefits should start when your claim is approved. (This is also the date used to pay you for a new disability or an increase in a disability!)

Step 2: Decide How to Submit

You have a few options for submitting your intent to file. Choose the one that feels easiest for you:

1. Online: The quickest way to submit is through the VA's website.

2. By Phone: Call the VA at 1-800-827-1000 and let them know you want to submit an intent to file.

3. By Mail: You can send in VA Form 21-0966, "Intent to File a Claim for Compensation and/or Pension, or Survivors Pension and/or DIC."

   a. If you ever mail anything to the VA, I highly recommend that you send it with tracking or signature confirmation if you use USPS.

Every call, every click, every envelope, you track it like mission-critical intel. I don't care if it's the VA, DFAS, or some clerk at a records center. You write down the date, time, the number you called, the name of the person you spoke to, how many times they bounced you around like a bad radio signal, and what they told you. If you mail something, note the postmark date and slap tracking on it. If you submit something online, screenshot the confirmation or print that page like it's an award certificate.

Because when things go sideways—and they might—you're going to need receipts, timestamps, and names. That paper trail is your weapon. Don't trust your memory or rely on luck. Document everything like your claim depends on it—because it sure does! If you have that database for your ailments (which you should!), consider adding a tab to track this type of communication.

When your claim is at eleven months of no movement and you have to call the main VA hotline, the White House VA line, or just the veterans' advocate, they will all ask you for these details. The more detailed you can provide, the more they will sit up and take notice!

Step 3: Submitting Online

If you're going the online route, here's a step-by-step guide:

1. Log In: Go to va.gov and log in using your DS Logon, My HealtheVet, or ID.me account.

2. Navigate: Find the section for "Compensation" and look for the option to start a new claim.

3. Because you were smart and already submitted your intent to file, you just have to complete your claim.

Step 4: Submitting by Phone

Prefer the personal touch? Here's what to do:

1. Dial In: Call the VA at 1-800-827-1000.

2. Tell them: Clearly state that you want to submit an intent to file for a VA disability claim.

3. Confirm Details: They'll ask for some basic info, like your name, Social Security number, and date of birth. Make sure everything's accurate.

Step 5: Submitting by Mail

If you love the feel of pen and paper, here's your path:

1. Download the Form: Go to va.gov and search for VA Form 21-0966, or you can find it on the https://boots2benefits.com/resources website.

2. Fill It Out: Complete the form with all necessary information. Be thorough!

3. Mail It: Send the completed form to the appropriate VA regional office. The address will be on the form or the VA's website.

4. *Please* keep a copy for yourself of what you mailed. Remember, annotate every communication with the VA!

5. Mail it by courier with a tracking number or via signature confirmation by USPS, FedEx, courier, stagecoach, etc!

Step 4: Submit Your Claim

When you're ready to file your claim, include the following:

1. VA Form 21-526EZ: This is your main application for disability compensation.

2. VA Form 21-4142: Authorization to disclose information.

3. VA Form 21-4142a: General release for additional medical providers.

4. Any Service Treatment Records: These will bolster your claim.

5. Option: Add a cover letter (see step 5).

Step 5: Include a Detailed Cover Letter

In your cover letter, explain that you've authorized the VA to obtain your civilian medical records. Outline where they can find every recorded annotation of the ailment in your military and civilian records (use that database). This will ensure they don't miss any of your important medical history. There is an example in Chapter 15.

The VA isn't playing around with these wait times

Step 6: Double-Check Everything

Before you send everything off, make sure all your forms are filled out correctly and completely, you've signed and dated them. Keep copies of everything for your own records.

Step 7: Submit Everything

After you have a copy, submit your claim packet via one of the following methods:

1. Online: Upload your forms on the va.gov website.

2. Mail: Send your forms to the appropriate VA regional office.

3.   In Person: Drop off your forms at a VA regional office or your local VSO office. (Do yourself a favor and take a selfie with the person who receives your packet!)

Step 8: Follow Up

After submission, stay on top of things:

1.   Check Status: Regularly check the status of your claim on va.gov.

2.   Whether you file by the internet, mail, or phone, you can call 1-800-827-1000 to check on the status of your claim processing if you feel it is taking too long. Keep a record of all the dates and times that you call for status.

3.   Respond Promptly: If the VA requests additional information or clarification, respond as quickly as possible.

CHAPTER 7: C&P EXAMS

Preparing for your C&P exam is crucial. This isn't just another appointment. Your C&P exam is the VA's version of a recon mission. They're showing up to assess the battlefield—*you*. And if you go in unprepared, you're giving them the high ground. Don't do that. Here's my comprehensive guide to get you mission-ready using your spreadsheet of ailments and the 38 CFR as your roadmap.

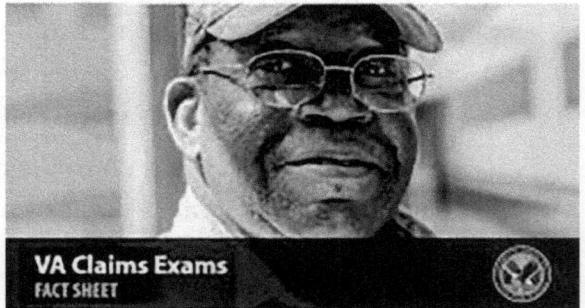

Don't be surprised but most of the C&P examiners are not veterans, nor do they genuinely know what to look for or what 38 CFR states about the ailment. This is your moment to shine!

BEFORE

Step 1: Review Your Ailments Spreadsheet

1. Compile Information: Gather your spreadsheet of ailments, including each condition, its symptoms, and how it affects you daily.

2. Document Severity: Note the severity of your symptoms and any functional limitations you experience, such as mobility issues, pain levels, or cognitive difficulties.

I know, we're all big, tough, squared-away soldiers, devil dogs, squids, and flyboys. We're all warriors but now is not the time, you must humble yourself and be real, true and honest. We've been trained to suck it up, push through, and not complain. But let me remind you of a hard-hitting truth: that mindset will wreck your VA claim.

You've got to humble yourself. Period. Stop making excuses. Drop the, "It's not that bad," and "Others had it worse," or "I don't want to seem weak." I heard and said it all myself. And guess what? The VA will take that silence and run with it. You've got to lay it all out—the good, the bad, and the ugly. You want to be honest and straightforward without sugarcoating it. If you can't sleep, if your back's toast, if your anxiety is through the roof, say so. Be direct. Be factual. You're not whining. You're not weak—you are a battle-worn warrior. You're finally speaking up for yourself. And that's one of the toughest damn things a warrior can do.

What most veterans don't realize as they start this process is a fact that bears repeating. When you finally get comfortable speaking your truth and win your claim, you become invaluable to other veterans who are still struggling with that warrior pride. Your breakthrough becomes their lifeline.

> This is what Sarge is saying: if you wake up with a migraine, don't blame the aged cheese you had for dinner, if it was truly a night filled with bad dreams, panic attacks, or pain. Be honest, don't find a less 'real' justification – this is the time to say it like it is!

Step 2: Familiarize Yourself with the 38 CFR

1. Identify relevant sections: Review the CFR manual (Title 38, Part 4) to identify the sections that pertain to your specific ailments. Pay attention to the criteria for assigning disability ratings and the symptoms listed for each condition.

2. I will bet my paycheck, hypothetically, that you will find symptoms of an ailment that you have, but you didn't know it was connected to 'that' ailment!

3. Know your rating: Understand the criteria for determining your percentage rating based on the severity of your symptoms and their impact on your daily life. You take that knowledge with you into the C&P exam.

4. Write down the percentage you believe you have earned based upon your symptoms. You need to take it into the C&P exam with you and ensure that examiner knows that you've researched and know what needs to be proven.

Step 3: Prepare Notes for the Exam

1. You *need* to go into the C&P exam with notes.

   a. Write down how an ailment affects you on your worst day. Vividly describe how you feel on your worst day, including the intensity of your symptoms and any exacerbating factors. This is not the time to "man up." Be humble and truthful.

   b. Work Impact: Explain how your ailments affect your ability to perform your job duties, including any accommodation you require, or workdays missed due to illness. (This can be if you called off work because your nightmares were so bad that you couldn't sleep and you are concerned you'll fall asleep on the forklift, driving to work, during a meeting, etc.)

c.   Home Life: Discuss how your conditions impact your activities of daily living at home, such as household chores, cooking, cleaning, and personal care tasks. Tell them how you are hyper-vigilant, and the kids don't understand why you always have to sit in the back of the restaurant with your back to the wall and your eyes on the room!

d.   Relationships: Describe how your ailments affect your relationships with family members, friends, and significant others, including any social or emotional challenges you experience.

2.   Military Medical Records: From your ailment database, provide specific details on where to find your extensive medical documentation in your military and civilian medical records, including the dates and locations of the doctor's notes related to your service-connected condition(s).

Step 4: Bring Supporting Evidence—Grab that ailment spreadsheet/ database!

1.   Medical Records: Bring copies of relevant medical records, including doctor's notes, test results, imaging studies, and treatment plans, to support your claims.

2.   Buddy Statements: If available, bring buddy statements from fellow service members or friends who can attest to the impact of your ailments on your daily life.

DURING

Step 5: Practice Self-Advocacy

1.   Be Assertive: Advocate for yourself during the exam by clearly articulating your symptoms, limitations, and how they impact your life. This is why you write it all down, so

you don't forget any of the symptoms you have that are outlined in 38 CFR.

2. Ask Questions: Don't hesitate to ask the examiner questions
    about the exam process or how your conditions are being
    evaluated.

3. Request Clarification: If you don't understand a question or
    need clarification, ask the examiner to repeat or rephrase it.

4. Educate them on the military culture, e.g., why you didn't go
    to sick call or report it

Let's take it up a notch. When you roll into that C&P exam, know
your rating *before* you walk in. I'm talking about 38 CFR—the VA's
own rulebook. You study that thing like it's your rifle manual. You
need to know what percentage your condition qualifies for based on
the symptoms, and if they don't ask? You better darn well *tell* them.
Don't wait for permission to speak up. They need to know you're
not just a patient, you're a well-informed veteran who knows the
regs front to back, sideways, and upside-down. Honestly, nine times
out of ten, my C&P examiners asked me where I thought I should be
rated and why.

Now lay it out for them. (Remember you have all of this written
down, so you don't miss anything!) Then you say, "According to 38
CFR, my condition qualifies for a 70% rating because I experience X,
Y, and Z." And then you detail the symptoms:

- If you don't sleep more than two hours at a time without
  waking up in a sweat? Say it.

- If you experience panic attacks in public that keep you from
  working? Say it.

- Tell them about the flashbacks that are so real you hit the
  deck at fireworks shows! Say. It. All.

And here's the part most folks miss: you take this time to educate that examiner. Tell them why you never went to sick call. Tell them how your platoon sergeant publicly shamed anyone who showed "weakness," called it malingering, made you run laps while sick, or handed out extra duty for "crybaby complaints." Make sure they understand that a hostile culture is why your medical record looks clean, but your body and mind are falling apart now.

Don't be silent. Be strategic. Be thorough. Be loud when you need to be. This is your war now!

Remember, every time you successfully advocate for yourself in that exam room, you're proving it can be done. When you walk out with the rating you deserve, don't keep that victory to yourself. Share your strategy. Help another veteran understand how to fight for themselves. That's the IGY6.2 way—we win together.

AFTER

Step 6: Follow Up After the Exam

1. Write it down: As soon as you walk out, document everything. What questions were asked, how long it lasted, anything the examiner said or did that seemed off. If something's fishy, you can challenge it later. (Use the talk-to-text feature on your mobile phone! Just talk through it and give every detail. You can clean it up later.)

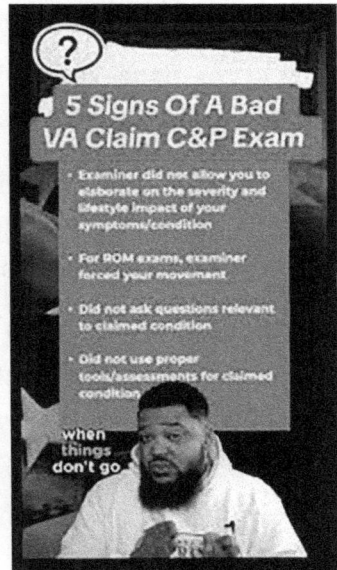

5 Signs Of A Bad VA Claim C&P Exam
- Examiner did not allow you to elaborate on the severity and lifestyle impact of your symptoms/condition
- For ROM exams, examiner forced your movement
- Did not ask questions relevant to claimed condition
- Did not use proper tools/assessments for claimed condition

when things don't go

2. Request Copies: Ask for copies of the C&P exam report and review it carefully to ensure that your symptoms and limitations are accurately documented.

Here's how you get your C&P exam results, because what that examiner wrote could make or break your claim.

You've got the right to request the C&P report under FOIA—the Freedom of Information Act—and you do it by filing VA Form 20-10206. That's your official ask for your C&P exam write-up. You can send it three ways:

- Use the *QuickSubmit Tool* online through va.gov (fastest route if you've got an account)

- *Fax it* to 844-531-7818

- Or go old-school and *mail it* to the VA Evidence Intake Center

Now, don't expect overnight magic. These things usually take twelve to eighteen weeks, but if your file is thick or the VA's backed up (which they usually are), it could take up to a year. Yeah, it's a slow march, but it's one worth making. You need that file to see exactly what the examiner documented, where they got it right, or where they screwed the pooch.

Stay in the fight, keep your own records, and always double-check what the VA puts in yours. This is how you take back control.

- Follow Up: If you have any concerns or discrepancies, follow up with the VA to address them and provide additional evidence if necessary.

By thoroughly preparing for your C&P exam and effectively communicating the impact of your ailments, you can ensure that your disability claim accurately reflects your level of impairment and receives a fair evaluation by the VA.

Let's go through this again – your checklist for your C&P Exam

1. Take your spreadsheet of ailments. Medical records are massive (typically). Tell them exactly where to find the military doctor notes in your records (by date and location).

2. Know what 38 CFR states (symptoms and percentage rating) and be prepared to share/support what the CFR states.

3. Know what percentage you are entitled to by the symptoms that are outlined in 38 CFR and tell the C&P examiner. Even if they don't ask, you tell them.

4. Take notes with you:

   a. How you feel on your worst day

   b. How it affects your work

   c. How it affects your home life

   d. How it affects your relationships

5. Educate the examiner on your military experiences and the environment.

When you master this C&P exam process and get the rating you've earned, you become part of something bigger. The IGY6.2 Movement is built on veterans like you who figured it out, then turned around to help the next warrior in line. Your success story becomes someone else's hope. That's how we ensure no veteran gets left behind. It's a mission worth completing.

PART III: REGULATIONS & TASKS

Just like when we were in the military, we followed regulations and protocols, such as being told which foot to lead with when we started to march. The VA claims process operates under the same structure. The great news is that understanding the 38 CFR can unlock countless resources for you while providing clarity on many confusing aspects of the process. We're going to explore this together to navigate this path ahead! When we are done, you will be filled with knowledge and (hopefully) feel empowered to move forward.

And never forget, when you master this 38 CFR knowledge and secure the rating you deserve, you become invaluable to other veterans who are still struggling to understand the system. Your hard-won expertise becomes someone else's lifeline.

CHAPTER 8: WARRIOR'S GUIDE 38 CFR

Consult 38 CFR – This is your second bible, as it provides wisdom and guidance! Study it, learn it, and know what percentage you 'should' have and *why* (what symptoms you display).

Check specifically for the appropriate percentage as listed in 38 CFR manual. It will break down how it relates to your specific ailment(s) and is the regulation that the VA will use to determine your disability rating.

Here's a breakdown of how to navigate 38 CFR and calculate your percentage rating based on the side effects you experience:

Step 1: Access the 38 CFR Manual

The CFR Title 38, Part 4, commonly referred to as the Schedule for Rating Disabilities, outlines the criteria used by the Department of Veterans Affairs to assign disability ratings for different medical conditions. You can access it online through the US Government Publishing Office website or various VA resources.

1. Any veteran can obtain a printed copy of 38 CFR by making a written application to the Department of Veterans Affairs

installation that has custody of the records or documents they wish to obtain. They must specify the particular record or document and the purpose for which the copy is needed. This process is also found on the Department of Veterans Affairs website.

2. If you don't want to wait, you can purchase it at https://bookstore.gpo.gov/catalog/code-federal-regulations-cfrs-print.

Allow Sarge to give a helpful hint here: Always double-check the printed version of 38 CFR with the eCFR online, as it is continuously updated.

Step 2: Identify Your Ailments

Review the CFR manual to identify the specific codes and criteria that correspond to your medical conditions. Each ailment is assigned a numerical code and a detailed description of the symptoms and severity levels associated with it.

Step 3: Understand the Rating Criteria

For each ailment, the CFR manual provides a rating schedule that outlines the criteria for assigning disability ratings based on the severity of symptoms and their impact on your ability to function. Ratings are typically assigned on a scale from 0% to 100%, with higher ratings indicating more severe impairment.

Step 4: Evaluate Your Symptoms

Carefully assess your symptoms and how they align with the criteria outlined in the CFR manual. Take note of any specific side effects or limitations you experience as a result of your medical conditions.

Step 5: Determine Your Percentage Rating

Based on your symptoms and their severity, determine the appropriate percentage rating according to the criteria specified in the CFR manual. Be thorough in documenting all relevant information and providing evidence to support your claim.

Step 6: Seek Professional Assistance if Needed.

If you're unsure about how to interpret the 38 CFR manual or calculate your percentage rating, consider seeking assistance from Sarge, a VSO, accredited agent, or attorney who specializes in VA disability claims. They can provide expert guidance and ensure that your claim is accurately evaluated.

Step 7: Submit Your Claim

Submit your claim to the VA along with supporting documentation and evidence. Be sure to include detailed medical records, buddy statements, use the verbiage from 38 CFR (even if you normally wouldn't say it in that way) and any other relevant information to strengthen your case.

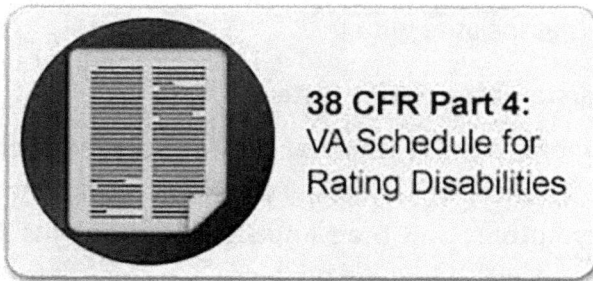

38 CFR Part 4:
VA Schedule for Rating Disabilities

Step 8: Follow Up and Advocate for Yourself

After submitting your claim, stay informed about its status and be prepared to advocate for yourself if necessary. If you disagree with the VA's decision or believe your rating is incorrect, you have the right to appeal and request a review of your case.

If you want to win this fight, you need to know the enemy's playbook—and that playbook is called the 38 CFR. Yeah, it isn't light reading, but it tells you exactly how the VA rates your conditions, the percentages, the symptoms, the side effects. It's all right there in black and white. And if you don't know it (which many veterans don't), they'll assess you however they deem appropriate.

Familiarize yourself with that manual like you're prepping for a mission. Match your ailments to what's listed. PTSD (Post-Traumatic Stress Disorder)? Joint pain? Sleep apnea? IBS (Irritable Bowel Syndrome)? Read the criteria and see where you fall. If you've got most or all of the symptoms tied to a 70% rating, then that's what you fight for, that is what you tell them—speak up for yourself.

Don't walk into the claims process blindly. You earned those benefits through service. Now it's time to secure them through strategy. Know your rights, know your rating, and speak the VA's language—38 CFR. That's how you win.

Remember, every time you successfully use 38 CFR to secure your proper rating, you prove it can be done. Don't keep that victory to yourself, share your strategy with other veterans. That's how the IGY6.2 Movement grows stronger, one successful claim at a time.

CHAPTER 9: NEXUS LETTERS

If your civilian doctor doesn't know how to write a Nexus letter, *you* do the research. *You* draft your Nexus letters for your civilian doctors! By composing the draft letter, you ensure that it includes all of the needed symptoms, key components, and verbiage that is outlined in the 38 CFR manual. There are plenty of examples of Nexus letters online, and I have included one at the end of this book. But remember to ensure that you communicate to the doctor that it is just a draft, and he/she can alter it to suit his/her medical needs. This is a helpful gesture, not a mandate.

Here's the bottom line, your doctor isn't getting paid a dime to write that Nexus letter—it's an extra chore on top of their already overloaded day. So, if you want to speed things up and not end up at the bottom of their "maybe later" pile, do the heavy lifting for them. Write the draft yourself. Include the facts, the timeline, the symptoms, and the connection to your service.

That way, all they need to do is review it, tweak it, put it on their letterhead, and sign their name. Trust me, if you hand them a ready-to-go draft, you'll get that letter back a heck of a lot faster than if you just say, "Hey, Doc, can you write something for the VA?" Work smarter, not harder. The more of the narrative you can control, the better strategy to win this war!

And, once again, your experience can benefit more than just you. When you master the art of drafting Nexus letters and get your claims approved, you become a veteran who can help others navigate this same process. Your expertise becomes inspiring to other veterans just starting their claims process.

VETERAN NEXUS

Step 1: When You Ask for a Nexus Letter, Ensure Your Doctors Understand the Importance of the Letter and Its Role in Your VA Claim.

1. Explain the VA disability process by providing a brief overview of how a Nexus letter can support your claim.

2. Describe your military service and give the doctor context about your military service, including any deployments, duties, or exposure to hazardous conditions.

3. Explain your TERA experience. You may have to give some background information on what TERA means in the VA world.

   Explain that TERA stands for Toxic Exposure Risk Activity. Sounds fancy, but in boots-on-the-ground terms, it means if you did something in service that exposed you to toxic junk—burn pits, jet fuel, chemical spills, contaminated water, radiation, you name it—and it's serious enough that it needed to be recorded in some kind of exposure tracking system, or the VA decides it's reasonable to link it to your military duties (that you need your Nexus letter to state), that's a TERA.

In short, if it messed with your health and it happened during your service to Uncle Sam, it counts. Whether they logged it in a database or the VA later agrees it's service-connected, TERA is the foundation for getting your claim for toxic exposure recognized. Don't let the acronym fool you, it's not just paperwork. It's the starting point for accountability.

Step 2: Provide Relevant Information

Equip your doctors with all the necessary information to write an effective Nexus letter:

1.   Medical history: Give a detailed account of your medical history related to your service-connected conditions. (Again, Sarge sounds like a broken record, but pull this information from your ailment spreadsheet/database.)

2.   Symptoms and limitations: Describe your symptoms (as per 38 CFR), how they affect your daily life, and any limitations they impose.

3.   Service connection: Clearly articulate how your current medical conditions are linked to your military service. Provide specific incidents, dates, and locations if possible.

4.   You can go as far as to provide the doctor with your service medical records so they have an opportunity to review them. (It's not your job to ensure they do, it's just your opportunity to offer it.)

Step 3: Template for Nexus Letter

Offer your doctors a template or guidance on what to include in the Nexus letter:

1.   Introduction: Start with a brief introduction, including your name, service branch, and dates of service.

2. Medical Opinion: Clearly state that the doctor is providing a medical opinion regarding the connection between your current condition(s) and your military service. Use the verbiage from 38 CFR in addition to the professional MSD (Merck, Sharp, and Dohme) manuals that civilian doctors use to diagnose and form medical opinions.

3. Detailed Explanation: Provide a detailed explanation of the medical condition(s), including diagnosis, onset, and progression.

4. Service Connection: Specifically state how the condition(s) are related to your military service. This is the crux of the Nexus letter and the doctor only has to write/state that "It is more likely than not" that it is connected to your military service.

5. Supporting Evidence: Reference any relevant medical records, test results, or statements from other health care providers that support the service connection.

6. Conclusion: Summarize the key points and reaffirm the doctor's opinion regarding the service connection.

Once you've successfully used this template approach to get your Nexus letters and win your claims, consider how you can help other veterans do the same. Share your template. Help a battle buddy understand the process. Remember IGY6.2, we succeed together.

See Chapter 15 for an example of a Nexus letter.

Step 4: Schedule an Appointment

Arrange a follow-up appointment with your doctors to discuss the Nexus letter:

1. Review the template: Go over the template or guidance you provided and ensure they understand what's required.

2.   Answer questions: Address any questions or concerns your doctors may have about writing the Nexus letter.

Step 5: Follow Up

After the appointment, follow up with your doctors to ensure they're able to provide the Nexus letter:

1.   Ask for an anticipated deadline, and try to allow the doctor to establish a reasonable deadline for receiving the letter. Don't be hesitant to let the doctor know that your claim is 'on hold,' with the VA claims clock ticking until they return the Nexus letter.

2.   Provide Assistance: Help in gathering any additional information or records they may need to complete the letter.

3.   Be clear that the doctor can and should edit, revise, rewrite, or completely rework the draft letter, however they see fit. Your draft is meant as a goodwill gesture to give them a starting point to respect their time. It is not your intention to put words in their mouth. They are medical professionals, and the final letter needs to reflect their expert diagnosis.

4.   Always get a copy of the letter!

This part's going to hit different, so be prepared to read the honest-to-goodness truth about your condition, plain and raw, right there in black and white. It isn't always easy to swallow, especially when it's a Nexus letter about your mental health. Seeing stuff like "social isolation," "emotional detachment," or "chronic anger" on paper can feel like a gut punch.

Look at it objectively, like a mission report. This isn't about pride, it's about facts, and those facts are what help you get the rating and treatment you need. Hand it off to someone who knows you best—your spouse, your mom, your adult kid—and ask, "Does this sound like me?" Their perspective might just confirm what you've been too tough to admit. That's not a weakness, that's honesty. And it's how you win this fight.

And like the other steps we have covered so far, always remember, when you master this Nexus letter process and secure the benefits you've earned, you become part of something bigger. Our IGY6.2 Movement is built on veterans like you who figured out the system, then turned around to help the next warrior in line. Your success story becomes someone else's inspiration.

CHAPTER 10: BUDDY STATEMENTS

You did not serve alone! There were plenty of military brothers and sisters with you! Plus, you had family, religious leaders, teachers, and civilian friends, too.

If you have a comrade, friend, or family that have inside knowledge, ask him/her to write a statement on your behalf. Similar to your doctors and the Nexus letter, if your buddy doesn't know how to do it, discuss it, draft it for them, and let them alter it to fit their voice.

> **Tips for Your VA Buddy Letter**
>
> 1. Ensure that the buddy letter is from someone credible and competent
> 2. Be sure to sign and date the buddy letter
> 3. Be concise
> 4. Include contact information
> 5. Include identifying information
> 6. Certify the buddy letter

Buddy statements are like the secret sauce of your VA disability claim—they add that extra flavor and depth that makes your case stand out.

Here's why they're so important:

1. Corroboration
2. Buddy statements provide additional evidence to support your claim. They corroborate your account of events, possibly the timeframe, injuries, or conditions during your mili-

tary service. Having witnesses strengthens the credibility of your claim.

3. Different Perspectives

This comprehensive approach helps paint a more accurate narrative of your service-related conditions.

4. Credibility

Having your battle buddy tell a very similar recollection will enhance the credibility of your claim. Testimonials from fellow service members, family, or friends carry weight with the VA, as they come from individuals who shared similar experiences and conditions. Their firsthand accounts lend credibility to your assertions.

5. Specific Details

Buddy statements can provide specific details about incidents or events that support your claim. Whether it's describing a combat situation, documenting exposure to hazardous substances, or recounting injuries sustained during training exercises, these details add substance to your claim.

This is the time to bring out the war stories—the real ones. Write it down—that time Sergeant Butthead made you stand in the rain for three damn hours because he thought it'd be funny punishment for forgetting to clean up the motor pool. You ended up with a foot fungus that never went away, and Corporal Smith got pneumonia so bad he looked like a science experiment gone wrong.

These aren't just old stories, they're evidence, even if you laugh about it now. They show where, when, and how you were exposed to things that jacked up your health during you time in service. So don't be shy. Now's the time to speak it out, write it down, and link it to your claim. You served. You endured. And now you deserve to be heard.

Remember, every detailed buddy statement you collect and every claim you win using these strategies makes you invaluable to other veterans who need witness testimony. Your success becomes someone else's saving grace.

6. Documentation

Buddy statements serve as documented evidence of your service-related conditions. They provide written records of witness testimony, which can be used to support your claim during the VA's evaluation process. Having written documentation strengthens the validity of your assertions.

7. Objective Witness

This type of statement comes from objective witnesses who have no personal stake in your claim. Buddy statements from other veterans carry more weight because they are from individuals who served alongside you and can provide unbiased testimony. You understand what details matter, what language works, and how to tell the truth in a way the VA understands, so you can always assist them with their statement.

8. Correlation with Medical Records

Buddy statements can complement your medical records by providing context and additional information. They can help bridge the gap between your documented medical conditions and the events or circumstances that caused them during your military service.

9. Human Element

Finally, buddy statements add a human element to your claim. They provide personal accounts of your experiences, struggles, and challenges during your military service. This human touch can resonate with VA adjudicators and help them understand the impact of your service-related conditions on your life.

Just remember, your battle buddies have your back. They understand the hardships of reporting ailments while on active duty. We all remember being yelled at in front of the whole platoon:

1.   Suck it up and drive on!

2.   Stop being a pu$$y—toughen up!

3.   You are just going to leave and let your squad fend for themselves?

4.   Put your nose to the grindstone!

I cannot say it enough, buddy statements play a vital role in strengthening your VA disability claim by providing additional evidence, different perspectives, and credibility to your assertions. Don't underestimate their importance. They can make a significant difference in the outcome of your claim.

PART IV: OPERATION AFTERMATH

Congratulations! You've successfully navigated the process and received that thick envelope in the mail that is your decision letter. So what are your next steps?

CHAPTER 11: DECISION LETTER

DEPARTMENT OF VETERANS AFFAIRS
810 Vermont Ave NW
Washington, D.C. 20420

July 1, 2021

John Michael Doe
5445 Honor Drive
Hope, AR 71802

In Reply Refer to:
xxx-xx-4321
27/eBenefits

Dear Mr. Doe,

This letter is a summary of benefits you currently receive from the Department of Veterans Affairs (VA). We are providing this letter to disabled Veterans to use in applying for benefits such as state or local property or vehicle tax relief, civil service preference, to obtain housing entitlements, free or reduced state park annual memberships, or any other program or entitlement in which verification of VA benefits is required. Please safeguard this important document. This letter is considered an official record of your VA entitlement.

Our records contain the following information:

Personal Claim Information

Your VA claim number is: xxx-xx-4321

You are the Veteran.

Military Information

Your most recent, verified periods of service (up to three) include:

Branch of Service	Character of Service	Entered Active Duty	Released/Discharged
Army	Honorable	September 17, 1990	June 22, 1996
Army	Honorable	June 23, 1999	May 5, 2005

(There may be additional periods of service not listed above.)

VA Benefit Information

You have one or more service-connected disabilities:	Yes
Your combined service-connected evaluation is:	100%
Your current monthly award amount is:	$4268.39
The effective date of the last change to your current award was:	January 1, 2021
You are considered to be totally and permanently disabled due solely to your service-connected disabilities:	Yes
The effective date of when you became totally and permanently disabled due to your service-connected disabilities:	December 15, 2004

It is imperative that you thoroughly read your decision letter, even if it says your disability was denied. It will still have valuable information, but it may seem like it's written in Greek. Have no fear, it will contain the roadmap to get you a higher rating. In the final few pages, the letter will detail what you need to prove so you can take additional steps, such as taking an injectable medication, to support that higher rating.

This letter will contain vital information regarding the ailment evaluated. You may have numerous ailments in one letter or just one ailment. Regardless, the letter will be quite lengthy. You still need to take the time to read it!

Within your letter, there is crucial information on how to appeal the decision (if it was denied or 'under' evaluated). Pay close attention to the decision information, as it will outline what you will need to prove to get to the next level of disability. It will also tell you if the VA found evidence to support it. Lastly, the mistake may be listed there too! Example is if they state that you were not in a TERA event but you have proof that you were stationed there. The disability level, based upon your symptoms for an ailment, is also located in 38 CFR.

This letter will help you navigate the next step in your claim process effectively and ensure you receive the benefits you earned. And here's something most veterans don't realize: When you master reading decision letters and successfully navigate the appeals process, you become invaluable to other veterans who are staring at their own confusing letters. The IGY6.2 Movement thrives on veterans who've been through this battle helping others decode their roadmap to success.

CHAPTER 12: APPEAL

Be prepared to say, "I do not agree" with the VA decision. If you don't, you don't, so respond! Tell them why! Every successful appeal you fight doesn't just win your benefits—it proves the system can be beaten when you know how to fight back. That knowledge becomes ammunition for the next veteran facing the same battle. That's the IGY6.2 way. Reiterate where to find the information in your military and civilian medical records. *Write* the letter from your notes you took to the C&P exam.

It's essential to be prepared to disagree with the VA decision if you believe it doesn't accurately reflect your circumstances. Here's how you can assert your rights and advocate for yourself effectively:

Step 1: Understand Your Rights

Know Your Options: Familiarize yourself with the appeals process and the different avenues available for challenging a VA decision. You have the right to appeal if you disagree with the outcome of your claim.

Step 2: Review the Decision Letter

Carefully Read: When you receive the decision letter from the VA, review it thoroughly to understand the rationale behind the decision and the evidence considered.

Step 3: Evaluate the Decision

1. Assess the Rationale: Determine whether the decision accurately reflects your medical conditions, symptoms, and limitations as documented in your medical records and supporting evidence.

2. Identify Discrepancies: Look for any discrepancies or errors in the decision that may have influenced the outcome of your claim.

3. This is where your C&P examination memorandum for record will come in handy. Since you made sure that you emailed it to yourself so it is date and timestamped, it will provide a clear outline of what happened (or didn't happen) during the C&P exam.

Step 4: Gather Additional Evidence

1. Seek Supporting Documentation: If you believe the VA overlooked important evidence or didn't adequately consider certain aspects of your case, gather additional medical records, buddy statements, or expert opinions to support your claim.

2. This is where the IGY6.2 Movement really shines. When you've successfully gathered evidence and won your appeal, you become the veteran who can guide others through the same process. The IGY6.2 Fund exists partly because not every veteran can afford the additional medical records or expert opinions needed for appeals. Your success becomes their hope.

Step 5: Prepare Your Appeal

1. File a NOD: If you decide to appeal the decision, file a Notice of Disagreement with the VA within the specified timeframe. This formally notifies the VA of your intent to challenge the decision.

2. Provide a Detailed Explanation: Clearly explain the reasons for your disagreement with the decision and provide any new evidence or information that supports your case.

3.　Consider Representation: You have the option to seek representation from a VSO, accredited agent, or attorney who can assist you with the appeals process and ensure your rights are protected.

Step 6: Stay Informed and Engaged

1.　Monitor Your Case: Stay informed about the status of your appeal and any updates from the VA. Follow up regularly to ensure your case is progressing.

2.　Advocate for Yourself: Don't hesitate to advocate for yourself throughout the appeals process. Be proactive in communicating with the VA and providing any additional information or documentation they may request.

Step 7: Exercise Your Right for a Hearing

Request a Hearing: If you're dissatisfied with the outcome of your appeal, you have the right to request a hearing before the Board of Veterans' Appeals (BVA). This allows you to present your case directly to a Veterans Law Judge.

Step 8: Seek Legal Assistance if Needed.

Consult with an Attorney: If you encounter challenges during the appeals process or believe your rights are being violated, consider seeking legal assistance from an attorney who specializes in VA disability law.

Remember, it's your right to disagree with the VA decision and to pursue an appeal if you believe it's warranted. Don't hesitate to assert your rights and advocate for the benefits you're entitled to based on your service-connected conditions. When you successfully navigate the appeals process and secure the benefits you deserve, don't keep that victory to yourself. Share your strategy. Help another veteran understand how to fight back. You can help the IGY6.2 Movement grow stronger.

IGY6

As a veteran, remember that you are never alone. Even in moments when you may feel isolated, you have a dedicated team standing beside you. In this section, we'll explore specific and specialized resources available to veterans, ensuring you have the support you need every step of the way.

It's very fitting for part 5 to be named, "I've got your six," which literally means "I've got your back" or "I support you." This phrase originates from the military clock system, where each position is represented as if you were standing in the center of the clock face. In this context, "6" refers to the 6:00 position, which is directly behind you. So saying "I've got your six too (IGY6.2)" indicates that B2B team is looking out for you and ensuring your safety from behind, emphasizing trust and mutual support within a team. Be reassured that we've got your back.

Boots 2 Benefits manages the IGY6.2 Fund. This fund was built on that very promise—that no veteran gets left behind, not in combat, not in life, and sure as heck not during their VA claims fight.

The IGY6.2 Fund is here to support our brothers and sisters when the system leaves them hanging. Can't afford a Nexus letter? Need help with document prep? Transportation to a C&P exam? We step in. This isn't charity, it's a continuation of service. We look out for each other, because we know what it's like to fight a war, come home, and start fighting a whole new one with the VA.

So, when you hear "IGY6.2," know that it's not just a slogan. It's a promise. The beauty of the IGY6.2 Fund is that it creates a cycle of support. When you receive your back pay from a successful claim, you have the opportunity to pay it forward—helping fund the next veteran's fight. Again, it's not about charity. It's about continuing the mission. We take care of our own because that's what we do. That's who we are. *You're not alone.* We've got your six. Always.

CHAPTER 13: MILITARY SEXUAL TRAUMA (MST)

Military Sexual Trauma (MST) can be experienced by both male and female service members. The VA uses this term to refer to a sexual assault or threatening sexual harassment experienced during military service. MST includes any sexual activity during military service in which you were involved against your will or when unable to say no.

This veteran condition causes occupational and social impairment characterized by a decrease in work efficiency and occasional periods of inability to perform some types of occupational tasks. As a result of a traumatic MST incident, one can experience life-altering symptoms such as anxiety, depression, sleep impairment, and even mild memory loss.

The VA looks for signs, events, or circumstances that provide some indication that a traumatic event happened. These markers may look like a dishonorable discharge, reduction in rank, Article 15s, drug use, patterns of poor conduct, and increasing the number of times you go to sick call.

There is a strong association with MST survivors in developing certain medical conditions such as obesity, weight loss, chronic pulmonary disease, liver disease, and hypothyroidism, along with mental health conditions such as bipolar disorders or schizophrenia.

Because MST claims usually lack traditional evidence, a person filing for a service-connected condition, mental illness, and/or a physical disability caused by MST can fill out VA Form 21-0781-A. The information requested on this form can help you supply the evidence you will need to prove your claim.

As the service member, you must provide as much proof as possible that the event happened and how the trauma plausibly contributed to your mental health disorder or other ailments. The third element must include a doctor's Nexus letter or opinion stating that your current condition or disability was likely or definitely caused by the military incident.

In addition to the existing hazards of military service faced by all service members, a female in the military is more likely to be raped by her teammate than killed by enemy fire. More than 45% of all women interviewed have experienced sexual assault or harassment while serving in the Armed Forces. Those who haven't been affected personally were keenly aware of its persistent threat. For some women, identifying as a veteran means opening themselves up to questions that remind them of their worst days.

And always remember that buddy statements are golden. Even if you did not report the MST incident to your Chain of Command, you may have mentioned it to a friend, parent, chaplain, or other people that may be able to write a statement on your behalf.

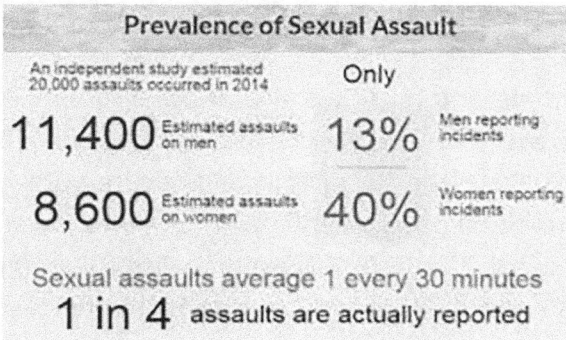

Prevalence of Sexual Assault

An independent study estimated
20,000 assaults occurred in 2014

Only

11,400 Estimated assaults on men

13% Men reporting incidents

8,600 Estimated assaults on women

40% Women reporting incidents

Sexual assaults average 1 every 30 minutes

1 in 4 assaults are actually reported

The IGY6.2 Movement is especially important for MST survivors. When you successfully navigate an MST claim and get the benefits you deserve, you become a beacon of hope for other survivors who are still struggling in silence. The IGY6.2 Fund exists partly because MST survivors often face additional barriers—they may not have traditional military networks, they may have been isolated during service, or they may lack the financial resources for Nexus letters and documentation. Your courage to file and win becomes someone else's permission to speak their truth.

CHAPTER 14: FEMALE VETERANS

My fellow female veterans, we are another breed, but also the same. I want every female veteran to understand that when you successfully navigate the VA system and secure your benefits, you become invaluable to other women veterans who are still fighting to be seen and heard. The IGY6.2 Movement isn't just about male camaraderie—it's about all veterans having each other's six, regardless of gender. Service women are told we are joining a brotherhood/sisterhood at enlistment, only to find out that women in the military oftentimes remain outsiders.

Throughout the United States history, female soldiers have served their country in a variety of military branches, various ranks, and roles. In honor of their service, the federal government provides a wide range of benefits for female veterans.

WOMAN VETERAN

Programs and Services for Women Veterans:

1. VA Health Care for Women

2. Center for Women Veterans

3. VA Benefits for Survivors of Military Sexual Trauma

4. Women Veteran-Owned Small Business Initiative

5. Maternity Care

6. Women Veteran Coordinators

Ever since the Revolutionary War, American women have made significant contributions and heroic sacrifices in service to their nation. Today, there are over two million veteran women in the United States. These brave women veterans have fought alongside men to keep America a free, safe country for generations to come.

Suppose you are a female veteran with a record of military service. In that case, you may be eligible to receive government benefits through many programs and services that meet the unique needs of women veterans.

Studies have demonstrated similar PTSD risk between male and female veterans. Still, compared to male veterans, female veterans experience fewer combat situations and are exposed to more military sexual trauma incidents. Many women veterans experience trauma, depression, anxiety, and develop eating disorders and mental health conditions. It's also found that they face many medical and social issues that affect their relationships and quality of life. Female veterans make up approximately 10% of the overall veteran population. But among women in America, only 1.5% are female veterans.

Female veterans are more likely to experience traumatic events such as sexual assaults and intimate partner violence. They are also associated with a higher risk for developing PTSD. The pros of being a female in the military are access to education and competitive benefits, while the cons include dealing with misogyny and increased risks of abuse.

Despite females' long-standing service, many female veterans struggle to feel recognized, respected, and valued as veterans. In civilian life, after completing their service, female veterans deserve the support and respect they have earned through serving their country.

The VA recognizes that female veterans face specific challenges and have unique healthcare needs. Legislation, such as the Women

Veterans Health Programs Act of 1992 and the Deborah Sampson Act of 2020, has enabled female veterans to expand gender-specific services and develop initiatives for eligible female veterans.

Female veterans often find themselves trapped in the misconception that they are not combat veterans. When they speak up about this experience, their service is frequently met with disbelief and devaluation, as if their contributions are somehow less valid. This narrative dismisses their sacrifices and undermines their status as veterans. While combat service is often glorified as the only true form of service, this viewpoint is problematic for several reasons. In reality, many male veterans did not serve in direct combat either. Yet for women who have served in combat roles, their contributions are often overlooked and undervalued.

This is where the IGY6.2 Movement becomes critical for female veterans. Every woman tears down the barriers for the next female veteran. The IGY6.2 Fund recognizes that female veterans often face unique challenges—from being questioned about their service to lacking traditional military networks for support. When you succeed, you pave the way for others.

Service women are acutely aware of their visibility as a minority while in uniform and their invisibility as female veterans once they enter the civilian world. To be a female in the military is to live with coexisting identities and thwart conventional gender roles. Although a female veteran may possess the greatest empowerment, she may also feel isolated, invisible, and misunderstood by both society and other veterans. This is one of the many reasons there are female veterans who choose not to self-identify as a veteran.

Unfortunately, the suicide rate for female veterans is 250% higher than that of the civilian population. The IGY6.2 Movement matters so much for female veterans. We cannot afford to lose any more of our sisters to a system that fails to recognize their service and sacrifice. When you get the help you need and the benefits you've earned, you become living proof that female veterans can win this fight. Your success becomes hope for another woman veteran who's considering giving up. Many veteran organizations don't feel the pressure to adapt for female veterans, and those organizations do not receive needed feedback on how they can improve the support they offer female veterans, as so many have given up trying.

Even though there are over two million female veterans currently living in the United States, many served in isolation and may have been the only female in their unit. This experience is re-lived in the veteran community.

There is hope on the horizon. Social media has been a very useful tool to help female veterans connect and recognize commonalities and experiences. Fortunately, there has been a rise in female veterans starting to self-organize to create safe spaces both on and off-line.

As a proud female veteran, I also have experienced many of the distasteful interludes mentioned in this chapter. Allow me to encourage all of the female veterans to reach out to me directly for support and assistance.

Remember, every female veteran who masters this system and secures her benefits becomes part of changing the narrative. The IGY6.2 Movement grows stronger when we include all veterans—male and female, combat and non-combat, MST survivors and those who served without trauma. We all served. We all earned our benefits. And we all deserve to have our six covered. That's what IGY6.2 means—no veteran left behind, period.

CHAPTER 15: CATCH ALL

There is so much information in *Boots 2 Benefits: Operation FUBAR.* But have no fear, additional Boots 2 Benefits books are in the works! And here's the beautiful thing about this growing library of resources, every veteran who successfully uses *Operation FUBAR* to win their claim becomes part of building the knowledge base for future books. Your experiences, your victories, your lessons learned all contribute to helping the next generation of veterans. That's the IGY6.2 way—we build on each other's success.

You can find the next book launch date at www.boots2benefits. com. A veteran can also seek assistance from the US Department of Veterans Affairs, retired Military Association websites, Veteran Service Organizations, personal finance advisors specializing in military benefits, local VA offices, and Military Transition Assistance Programs (TAPs).

VA Math

Although logical, a veteran cannot just add up all of their individual disability ratings. That is commonsense math, but it is *not* VA disability math! Go to this link for a clearer understanding: https://www. va.gov/disability/about-disability-ratings/

Resources, Forms, Links, and FUTURE BOOKS

There is so much information that you can find on the www. Boots2Benefits.com website. But if you want more one-on-one assistance, feel welcome to request a consultation. Find information on:

Future books:

1. Operation Advocate

2. Operation Caregivers

3. Operation Civilian

4. Operation Families

5. Operation Female

6. Operation K-9

Each of these upcoming books represents real needs identified by veterans who've been through the process. When you master *Operation FUBAR* and secure your benefits, consider how your experience could help shape these future resources. The IGY6.2 Movement grows stronger when veterans share their specialized knowledge, whether it's about caregiving, transitioning to civilian life, or supporting military families.

1. Forms:

   a. FOIA Request for C&P Exams

   b. Request military medical records

   c. Request civilian medical records

   d. Request a correction to your DD-214

2. Links:

   a. Request your DD-214

   b. Request your C-File

3. Resources:

   a. https://www.va.gov/

   b. https://www.myhealth.va.gov/mhv-portal-web/home

   c. https://www.va.gov/disability/how-to-file-claim/

    d.   https://www.woundedwarriorproject.org/programs/benefits-services

Remember, every resource you successfully use to win your claim becomes a tool you can share with other veterans. The IGY6.2 Fund exists partly because not every veteran has access to internet, transportation to VA offices, or the knowledge to navigate these resources alone. When you master these tools, you become invaluable to veterans who are still struggling to find their way.

Retirement Pay (DoD) vs. VA Disability

If you're retired, your retirement pay comes from the Department of Defense (DoD)—that's the paycheck you earned after years of standing the line. But disability pay? That's a whole different beast—it comes from the VA, not the DoD. Two different agencies, two different funding sources, and sometimes, two different sets of rules that don't play well together.

Now, here's where it gets tricky: Depending on what kind of retirement you've got (medical, length-of-service, etc.), and what type of disability rating you've been awarded, your payments could offset each other, or in some cases, not be affected at all. That's why you've got to be careful. Don't guess. Don't assume. This is where things get personal and complicated fast.

So, listen to me loud and clear: Sarge will not give any guidance or advice. Please get professional guidance. This is your livelihood we're talking about. Go to the experts at DFAS—the Defense Finance and Accounting Service. They know the ins and outs of how retirement pay and VA disability interact. Hit up https://www.dfas.mil, get the facts, and protect your pay. You earned every dollar, so make sure you keep them.

When you successfully navigate both your VA disability claim and understand how it interacts with your retirement pay, you become a valuable resource for other retiring veterans. The IGY6.2 Movement includes helping veterans understand these complex financial intersections. Your knowledge could be used as the key to financial security for a fellow veteran.

SAMPLE TEMPLATES

Create a personalized letter to accompany your claim submission that provides exact details of your military medical and specifics about the continued treatment by civilian doctors after leaving military service.

These templates have been battle-tested by veterans who've successfully used them to win their claims. When you customize these templates and achieve victory, consider sharing your successful approach with other veterans. The IGY6.2 Movement thrives on proven strategies that work.

Below is a sample template for this letter:

[Your Name]   [Date]
[Your Address]   Department of Veterans Affairs
[City, State, Zip Code]   [Regional Office Address]
[Your Phone Number]   [City, State, Zip Code]
[Your Email Address]

REFERENCE: [Add Your Claim Number and/or SSN]

Dear Claims Adjudicator,

Good day. I am writing to submit my claim for disability compensation based on service-connected conditions related to my military service. Enclosed, you will find my completed application form and supporting documentation, along with this letter providing additional information.

Firstly, I want to direct your attention to my military medical records, which can be found in the following location:

(Specify where your military medical records can be found, such as "My complete military medical records are on file with the Department of Defense and can be accessed electronically through the Defense Medical Information System (DMIS) at [insert website if applicable].")

These records comprehensively document the medical care I received during my time in the military, including any injuries, illnesses, or conditions that are relevant to my disability claim. I have ensured that all pertinent information is included and accessible for your review.

Additionally, I want to provide information about the civilian health care providers who have treated me for my service-connected conditions since my separation from the military. The following doctors and medical facilities have comprehensive records of my ongoing care:

** [Name of Civilian Doctor or Medical Facility]
[Address]
[Phone Number]
[Brief Description of Treatment Received]

** [Name of Another Civilian Doctor or Medical Facility, if applicable]
[Address]
[Phone Number]
[Brief Description of Treatment Received]

I have authorized these health care providers to release my medical records to the Department of Veterans Affairs for the purpose of evaluating my disability claim. Enclosed, you will find copies of the authorization forms I have completed for each provider.

In conclusion, I want to express my sincere gratitude for your attention to my claim. I understand the importance of providing comprehensive and accurate information to support my case, and I am confident that the enclosed documentation will assist you in your evaluation process.

Please do not hesitate to contact me if you require any further information or clarification regarding my claim. I am available at your convenience and eager to assist in any way I can.

Thank you for your time and consideration.

Sincerely,
[Your Name]
[Rank & Status (Retired or Veteran)]
[Branch of Service]
[SSN]

NEXUS LETTER TEMPLATE

Don't forget to ask that the Nexus letter be placed on the medical professional's letterhead.

[Your Name]
[Your Address]
[City, State, Zip Code]
[Your Phone Number]
[Your Email Address]
[Date]

Subject: Medical Nexus Opinion for Mr. [Veteran's Full Name]
Reference: C-File #[Insert] or Social Security Number #[Insert]

To Whom It May Concern at the Department of Veterans Affairs:

I am submitting this Independent Medical Expert (IME) opinion on behalf of Mr. [Veteran's Name], who is seeking service connection for midly severe obstructive sleep apnea (OSA) as a secondary condition related to his documented in-service diagnoses of PTSD, allergic rhinitis, and a deviated nasal septum.

As a licensed [Medical Specialty] with clinical experience in sleep disorders and respiratory pathophysiology, I have reviewed Mr. [Veteran's Name]'s complete medical file, including service treatment records, post-service medical evaluations, and the diagnostic findings from a sleep study conducted on June 12, 2024. I also conducted a personal medical evaluation of the veteran.

Mr. [Veteran's Name] served honorably in the [Branch of Service] from August 7, 1987, to October 28, 1998, during which time he was diagnosed and treated for allergic rhinitis and deviated septum, both of which were noted in his medical service records. Treatments included prescribed medications and nasal sprays to manage persistent nasal congestion and airflow obstruction.

The 2024 sleep study confirms a diagnosis of moderate obstructive sleep apnea, with documented episodes of upper airway collapse and disrupted sleep cycles. These clinical findings are consistent with well-established medical research linking upper airway obstruction—particularly due to chronic nasal blockage—to obstructive sleep apnea. It is my medical opinion that the veteran's nasal obstruction is a significant contributing factor to his OSA, and it is more likely than not (greater than 50% probability) that the OSA is secondary to the nasal conditions incurred and treated during his military service.

Research consistently demonstrates that nasal obstructions increase resistance to airflow, promote oral breathing, and heighten the risk of pharyngeal collapse during sleep—all key contributors to obstructive sleep apnea. In this case, the veteran's service-connected allergic rhinitis and deviated septum meet these criteria and provide a direct physiological link to his OSA.

Therefore, it is my professional medical opinion that Mr. [Veteran's Name]'s obstructive sleep apnea is more likely than not secondary to, and aggravated by, his service-connected nasal obstruction and allergic rhinitis.

Should you require any additional documentation or clarification, I am available to provide further medical insight as needed.

Sincerely,
[Signature]
[Medical Professional's Full Name]
[Credentials, Board Certifications]
[Medical License #]
[Phone Number | Email Address]

Bottom line: *Operation FUBAR* gives you the tactical knowledge to win your VA disability claim. But remember, this isn't just about your individual victory. Every veteran who masters these strategies and secures their benefits becomes part of the IGY6.2 Movement. You become the veteran who can guide others through the process, contribute to the IGY6.2 Fund when you receive your back pay, and help ensure no veteran gets left behind.

You served with honor. You earned these benefits. Now go file with confidence, win your claim, and when you succeed, turn around and help the next veteran in line. That's what IGY6.2 means. That's how we take care of our own. Always.

VOCABULARY

1. 38 CFR: Stands for Title 38 of the <u>Code of Federal Regulations</u> (CFR). It specifically relates to pensions, bonuses, and veterans' relief. This title contains the codified federal laws and regulations concerning military veterans' relief, pensions, and bonuses.

2. Buddy Statements: Buddy statements provide additional evidence to support your claim. They corroborate your account of events, injuries, or conditions during your military service. Having multiple witnesses strengthens the credibility of your claim.

3. C&P Exam: Compensation and Pension Exam. Think of it as your chance to show off your battle scars (literal or metaphorical).

4. Medical Records: Every doctor's visit, every prescription, every little "ouch" and "ugh" needs to be documented. The VA loves details.

5. Mental Health: Are your stress levels through the roof, or do you feel like you're constantly walking on eggshells? Service-related mental health conditions like PTSD are valid reasons to file.

6. Nexus Letter: This allows a civilian medical professional to provide a brief overview of your ailment (that is related to your military service), how it is being treated, what symptoms you are experiencing, and even some of your triggers. Clearly state that the doctor is providing a medical opinion regarding the connection between your current condition(s) and your military service.

7. NOD: Notice of Disagreement. This is what you file if the VA's decision makes you want to pull your hair out.

8. P&T: 100% Permanent and Total (P&T) VA disability rating means a veteran's service-connected disabilities are considered completely disabling and unlikely to improve, resulting in the highest level of VA disability benefits. The term "total" indicates the disability is severe enough to prevent substantially gainful employment, while "permanent" means the VA does not expect the condition to improve.

9. Physical Ailments: Do you have aches and pains that make you groan louder than your grandpa's old recliner? If you've got injuries or conditions from your time in service, that's a solid reason to file.

10. Private Medical Records: Don't forget any treatments you received outside the VA system.

11. Service Connection: Clearly articulate how your current medical conditions are linked to your military service. Provide specific incidents, dates, and locations if possible.

12. Service Records: These are like your superhero origin story. They prove you were there, did that, and got the T-shirt.

13. Service Treatment Records: These are the chronicles of every time you visited the medic or doctor while in service.

14. Service-Connected: This means your condition is directly related to your military service. The VA loves this term, so get comfy with it.

15. TERA, aka, Toxic Exposure Risk Activity: TERA is any military activity where a service member was likely exposed to harmful substances like burn pits, asbestos, jet fuel, contaminated water, radiation, industrial solvents, and chemical weapons agents. By VA definition, it is any activity that requires an entry in an exposure tracking record system, or one that the

VA determines is reasonably linked to a potential service-connected health condition.

16. Unemployability: Means a veteran is unable to maintain substantially gainful employment due to service-connected disabilities, even if their combined disability rating is less than 100%. This allows them to receive compensation at the 100% rate through the Total Disability based on Individual Unemployability (TDIU) program.

17. VA Medical Records: If you've been treated at a VA facility, grab these.

18. VSOs: These folks are like the GPS for your VA claim journey. They can help you understand if you have a case and guide you through the process.

19. VA Representatives: They're there to help too. Schedule a chat and ask all your burning questions.

Master these terms, and you become the veteran who can translate VA-speak for others. Every successful claim you file using this vocabulary makes you invaluable to the next veteran who's drowning in acronyms and regulations. That's the IGY6.2 way—your knowledge becomes someone else's lifeline.

VETERANS HELPING VETERANS

Please, allow me to encourage all of you to help another veteran! Sharing knowledge and supporting fellow veterans is crucial for ensuring success in navigating the VA disability claims process. Here are some ways veterans can share their knowledge and help each other:

1. Veterans Service Organizations (VSOs)

    a. Encourage fellow veterans to connect with reputable VSOs like the DAV, The American Legion, and Veterans of Foreign Wars.

    b. Share information about the services offered by VSOs, such as free assistance with VA benefits claims, representation in appeals, and advocacy for veterans.

2. Online Forums and Social Media Groups

    a. Recommend online forums and social media groups where veterans can share experiences, ask questions, and offer support to one another.

    b. Participate in discussions, provide helpful tips and advice based on personal experiences, and offer encouragement to veterans going through the claims process.

3. Local Veterans Community

    a. Encourage veterans to connect with their local veteran community through events, meetings, and gatherings.

b. Share information about local resources, support groups, and veterans' organizations where veterans can find assistance and camaraderie.

4. Peer Support Networks

a. Facilitate peer support networks among fellow veterans who have successfully navigated the VA disability claims process.

b. Organize informal meetings or group sessions where veterans can share tips, strategies, and share best practices for filing claims and appeals.

5. Mentorship Programs

a. Participate in mentorship programs where experienced veterans provide guidance and support to those who are new to the claims process.

b. Offer to mentor fellow veterans, share insights gained from personal experiences, and provide encouragement and assistance as needed.

6. Information Sharing

a. Share educational resources, articles, and guides related to VA benefits claims and appeals with fellow veterans.

b. Help veterans stay informed about updates to VA policies, procedures, and regulations that may impact their claims.

7. IGY6.2 Movement Participation

a. When you successfully navigate your claim using the strategies in this book, become an active part of the IGY6.2 Movement by sharing your victory story.

    b.   Consider contributing to the IGY6.2 Fund once you receive your back pay, helping other veterans access the resources they need.

    c.   Remember, every veteran you help becomes another success story that proves the system can be beaten when we work together.

By actively sharing knowledge, offering support, and fostering a sense of community among fellow veterans, individuals can empower one another to navigate the VA disability claims process successfully and achieve the deserved outcomes. Together, veterans can leverage their collective experiences and expertise to advocate for their rights and access the benefits they deserve and earned.

FEEDBACK

Make the next Boots 2 Benefits book better! Feel free to provide your suggestions, feedback, or items you'd like addressed in the next edition! Reach out to Sarge at Sarge@boots2benefits.com or check out her YouTube channel at "Ask Sarge" B2B Ask Sarge – YouTube.

BONUS BOOTS: OPERATION EXTRAS

All right, Troop, let's cut through the noise.

In my heart of hearts, I want this book—and every video on my YouTube channel—to empower you to fight this fight yourself. Period. You have got the grit, the experience, and now the tools to take charge of your own claim.

However, if after all that, you still feel like you need a little extra fire support, the Boots 2 Benefits team is standing by and ready to roll. We've got your six—no shame, no judgment, just boots-on-the-ground help from folks who've walked the same path.

Dealing with military medical paperwork is a full-on ambush. The regs are a mess, the systems are clunky, and the VA is not exactly handing out cheat sheets. So, feel free to call in support. Let the Boots 2 Benefits (B2B) team do the heavy lifting for you. We're a veteran-led unit, locked and loaded to give you personalized support that's tailored to your situation, not some one-size-fits-all nonsense.

We're not just paper-pushers—we're mission planners. B2B offers:

- One-on-one tutoring so you understand exactly what the VA's looking for
- Expert-level research to link your conditions to your service
- And strategic prep to get you ready for that C&P exam like it's your next deployment

We know what it feels like to be overwhelmed, overlooked, and outgunned by the system. We've been there. That's why we're committed to guiding you every step of the way—so you never go into this fight alone.

And if cost is a barrier, don't worry, we've got a plan for that too. That's where the IGY6.2 Fund comes in. "I Got Your Six" isn't just a motto; it's a mission. This fund helps cover deferred compensation and pro bono work for veterans who need help but can't afford it right now. If you're in the fight and funds are tight, we're still going to show up for you. Because no veteran gets left behind.

Visit us at www.Boots2Benefits.com to see how we can help you claim the benefits you earned through service and sacrifice. Need backup now? Reach out to me—Sarge—directly at Sarge@boots2benefits.com. Want more tips and tough talk? Head over to YouTube and check out "Ask Sarge" B2B Ask Sarge – YouTube.

Remember, every dollar you invest in getting your claim right the first time, every successful rating you secure, every appeal you win—it all contributes to something bigger. When you receive that back pay, consider paying it forward through the IGY6.2 Fund. Help the next veteran who's where you were when you first picked up this book. That's how we change the game—one successful claim, one helped veteran, one IGY6.2 contribution at a time.

You've got the tools. You've got the knowledge. You've got the strategy. Now go win this fight. And when you do, remember to reach back and pull up the next veteran behind you. That's not just good karma—that's the IGY6.2 promise. We succeed together, or we don't succeed at all. *Hooah!*

You served your country. Now let us serve you. IGY6.2—Always.

EPILOGUE

You made it to the end of this book! That says something about you. I hope you're walking away feeling empowered, prepared, and fired up to take charge of this VA claims process. Because as with everything we did in uniform, success starts when you step up and own the mission.

Remember this: We're veterans. We're part of the IGY6.2 team, and that means we've got each other's backs. The brotherhood and sisterhood doesn't end when you ETS (Expiration Term of Service) or retire—it evolves. Stay connected with other veterans, link up with support groups, and lean into the camaraderie you miss. That unspoken bond? You can reconnect with it through fellow veterans and showing up for each other like we always have.

When you successfully navigate this process and get the benefits you deserve, you become living proof that it can be done. Your victory becomes hope for another veteran who's ready to give up. That's how we grow stronger, one successful claim at a time.

The VA is always changing its rules, policies, and rating systems. Keep pushing forward. Stay sharp. Check in regularly at www.Boots2Benefits.com for updates, new tools, and tactical guidance.

You've got the resilience, the training, and the heart—or you wouldn't be a veteran. Now it's time to fight for you. And once you've got your boots planted firmly on the path? Reach back. Pull another veteran forward.

Thank you. You served this nation with honor. Now it's the VA's duty to serve you. Claim your benefits. You earned them.

Never forget—IGY6.2 Always.

🎖 ~Sarge

ACKNOWLEDGMENTS

Nobody crosses the finish line alone. Every mission, every break-through, every hard-earned victory comes with a squad of unsung heroes—the ones holding the line when things got tough and pushing me forward when I started to drag.

I've got an entire fire team—and then some—to thank. These warriors, mentors, and friends showed up when it mattered most, and I am eternally grateful for their support, wisdom, and heart:

1. **Dr. Joshua Okundaye, MA, LCSW-C, LICSW**: For helping me fight the battle within and showing me that healing is tactical.

2. **Dr. Michael Frazier, LTC, US Army (Ret.)**: My friend for over three decades. Thank you for walking this road with me.

3. **CPT Kabir Tompkins, Sr., Army Veteran**: For always leading with strength, integrity, and that steady command presence.

4. **Peter F. Murphy, former President of the Board of Charles County Commissioners,** a steadfast advocate for veteran services who supported critical veteran initiatives throughout Charles County.

5. **Taylor-Louise of Storybook Therapy, LLC**: For helping put words to wounds and turning pain into purpose.

6. **COL Eric B. Bryson, US Army (Ret.)**: While he was deployed, I maintained operations on the home front with our sons. With my Boots 2 Benefits mission and completing Operation FUBAR, his tactical support and expertise proved mission critical.

To all of you, thank you. You stood in the gap so I could stand up and speak for others.

The mission is accomplished and wouldn't have happened without you.

ABOUT THE AUTHOR

"Sarge" Julie Muster Bryson was born in Akron, Ohio, and answered the call to serve straight out of high school, enlisting in the US Army in 1987. She proudly served eleven years, wearing multiple hats across the force: Executive Administrative Assistant, Report of Survey Clerk, Orderly Room NCOIC (Noncommissioned Officer in Charge), Supply Sergeant, Small Group Instructor, and Property Book NCOIC. She did the work, led from the front, and never once backed down from a challenge.

Her final assignment landed her with the 226th Medical Battalion in Pirmasens, Germany, but she also operated out of Landstuhl, Babenhausen, and Giessen. She pulled overseas duty in South Korea (1991–1992) and stateside at Fort Jackson, SC; Fort Lee, VA; and Redstone Arsenal, AL. She served as cadre at the Ordnance NCO Academy, earned Fort Lee Soldier of the Year (1991), and was awarded the Meritorious Service Medal. In 1993, she graduated with distinction from BNCOC (Basic Noncommissioned Officer Course) and served as Student First Sergeant for her class.

Sarge didn't stop there. Her sons followed suit—both younger sons in USMC JROTC, and her oldest son went on to serve honorably as a United States Marine on active duty, both stateside and overseas.

In 2015, while she was employed at Charles County Government, under the leadership and guidance of the President of the Board of Commissioners, Peter F. Murphy, Sarge developed avenues to support the county's veterans. She put her nose to the grindstone, rolled up her sleeves and got to work for local veterans. Under the leadership of the President Commissioner, she created real, boots-on-the-ground change: founding the Veterans Corner, launching the Charles County Commission for Veterans Affairs (CVA), becoming the county's first Veteran Services Manager, and establishing a veteran hiring preference policy. She served as CVA liaison from 2018–2023, and after retiring in October 2023, she returned as a CVA Commissioner and Vice-Chair.

She is a lifetime member of the American Legion, Disabled American Veterans, and the Women's Veterans Memorial, and an active member of Women Veterans Interactive and Women Veterans Alliance. She also proudly serves on Senator Chris Van Hollen's US Military Academy Selection Board as an interviewer, helping shape the next generation of military leaders.

Sarge began helping veterans pro bono and one-on-one with their VA disability claims many years ago. What started as handouts and step-by-step guidance quickly grew into something bigger, this very book: *Boots 2 Benefits: Operation FUBAR.*

To carry that mission forward, Sarge launched Boots 2 Benefits, LLC, a consulting company focused on veteran advocacy. Through personalized services, strategy sessions, and full-spectrum claim support, Sarge and her team are helping fellow veterans take back control of the benefits they've earned. Her crew also produces "Ask Sarge," a boots-on-the-ground YouTube series that breaks down the VA process in plain English and keeps veterans in the fight.

www.ingramcontent.com/pod-product-compliance
Lightning Source LLC
Chambersburg PA
CBHW032100020426
42335CB00011B/424